Contents

MANYSAINTS
MANYWAYS

Multiple Intelligences Activities for Grades 1 to 6

MANYSAINTS MANYWAYS

PHYLLIS VOS WEZEMAN

ANNA L. LIECHTY

ave maria press   Notre Dame, IN

© 2003 by Ave Maria Press, Inc.

International Standard Book Number: 0-87793-973-X

Cover and Text design by Brian C. Conley

Printed and bound in the United States of America.

Library of Congress Cataloging-in-Publication Data
   Wezeman, Phyllis Vos.
     Many saints, many ways : multiple intelligences activities for grades
   1 to 6 / Phyllis Vos Wezeman, Anna L. Liechty.
       p. cm.
   Includes index.
    ISBN 0-87793-973-X (pbk.)
    1. Christian saints--Biography. I. Liechty, Anna L. II. Title.
   BR1710 .W45 2003
   268'.432--dc21

                                                            2002152567
                                                                CIP

To Dr. L. Edward Phillips and Rev. Sara Webb Phillips—Ed and Sara,
. . . thanks for your faithfulness in sharing God's love. P.V.W.

To the Wisecup children: Marie, Madeleine, Sarah, Nathalie, and Paul,
. . . my great-nieces and great-nephew who are saints in the making. A.L.L.

Special Thanks
To Judith Harris Chase . . .
. . . for contributing ideas for many of the learning activities in this resource.

INTRODUCTION

Stories of the lives of the saints have inspired writers and their readers since the beginning of Christianity. Resources about biblical, historical, and contemporary people of faith crowd the aisles of bookstores, line the shelves of libraries, and fill the pages of websites. Why, then, would anyone need to publish yet another book about the saints? The answer is simple: The stories of the saints deserve to be kept alive and fresh for readers in each generation.

As today's educators discover more about how learning takes place, new approaches enrich old methods. One recent theory has inspired great changes in educational practices. Howard Gardner, educational research professor at Harvard Graduate School of Education, introduced the concept of "Multiple Intelligences" to explain the ways that people learn. This theory has been readily embraced by religious and secular school systems as a model to incorporate into all classrooms. By applying the concept of Gardner's Multiple Intelligences Theory, this book attempts to find meaningful applications of "old" stories of faith to "new" situations and challenges of life.

Based on the stories of twelve biblical and historical saints—one per month—this resource offers information on the saint's lives as well as their legacy, using lessons centered around eight ways that people learn. Gardner proposes, based on his research, that each person possesses at least eight intelligences, eight distinct ways to learn and know about reality. These are:

- Bodily/Kinesthetic
- Interpersonal/Relational
- Intrapersonal/Introspective
- Logical/Mathematical
- Musical/Rhythmic
- Naturalist
- Verbal/Linguistic
- Visual/Spatial[1]

Each of the eight intelligences is explained on pages 10-13, including a summary of the specific way of knowing, how people with a specific intelligence learn, and what methods should be used to teach learners with a particular intelligence.

To tell the stories of the twelve saints highlighted in this book from January to December—each chapter contains nine parts. It begins with an overview of the life of the saint. In addition, eight activities—based on Gardner's Multiple Intelligences—explore the lessons about and from each person of faith. Sample activities for each of the eight intelligences include:

- Bodily/Kinesthetic—Dance/Gesture/Movement, Drama/Clown/Mime, and Puppetry
- Interpersonal/Relational—Culinary and Games
- Intrapersonal/Introspective—Creative Writing and Prayer
- Logical/Mathematical—Games
- Musical/Rhythmic—Music and Rhythm Stories
- Naturalist—Architecture and Photography
- Verbal/Linguistic—Storytelling
- Visual/Spatial—Art and Banners/Textiles

---

[1]Gardner, Howard. *Frames of Mind: The Theory of Multiple Intelligences.* New York: Basic Books, 1985.

Every lesson plan is organized into three parts: *Learn*, *Locate*, and *Lead*. The "Learn" portion offers a short description of the theme of the activity and describes what the students will experience. The "Locate" portion provides a list of supplies and preparations needed in order to present the learning challenge. In "Lead," directions for successfully guiding a group through the design are shared.

Multiple Intelligences Theory

"Learning Styles" is not a new concept in education, including religious education. Teachers have known for years that students learn in different ways—especially through auditory, visual, and kinesthetic experiences. An anonymous quote reminds the educator that people learn by hearing, seeing, and doing: "I hear—I forget; I see—I remember; I do—I understand."

Other statistics suggest that people learn:

- 10% of what they read
- 20% of what they hear
- 30% of what they see
- 50% of what they both see and hear
- 70% of what is discussed with others
- 80% of what they experience personally
- 95% of what they teach to someone else.

Because of recent work by Howard Gardner and others, the buzz word for "Learning Styles" has become "Multiple Intelligences." Gardner defines intelligence as "the ability to solve problems or fashion products that are of consequence in a particular cultural setting." Intelligence is not a static reality that is fixed at birth. It is a dynamic, ever-growing, changing reality throughout one's life. Intelligence can be improved, expanded, and amplified. The only limits to one's intelligence seem to be individual beliefs about what is possible.[2]

It is important to remember that the eight ways of knowing, the multiple intelligences, are interconnected. Each person has preferred ways of acquiring and processing information, but the best learning takes place when the student experiences learning in all eight ways, that is, when teaching methods include integration of the two sides of the brain—left and right—into a unified whole—the whole brain.[3]

Information about each of Gardner's eight intelligences is provided here as a tool for catechists to use in religious education settings. Each intelligence is summarized as a specific way of knowing with information about the way a person processes information. Finally, the section provides suggestions for learning activities for each intelligence.[4] Use the information and ideas as springboards to help students learn through all of their God-given capacities.

Bodily/Kinesthetic Intelligence

Bodily/Kinesthetic Intelligence is the capacity to use one's whole body to express ideas and feelings and the facility to use one's hands to produce or transform things.

People with Bodily/Kinesthetic Intelligence learn by becoming physically involved with the information to be learned. They need to move or manipulate objects to have a successful learning experience. Bodily/Kinesthetic Intelligence requires "learning by doing." Too much sitting or inactivity will cause this student to tune out.

Suggested methods to teach Bodily/Kinesthetic Intelligence include:

---

[2]Ibid.

[3] Lazear, David. *Seven Ways: The Artistry Of Teaching With Multiple Intelligences* and *Seven Ways Of Knowing: Teaching For Multiple Intelligences*. Palatine, IL: IRI/Skylight Training and Publishing, Inc., 1991.

[4] Bruce, Barbara. *7 Ways Of Teaching The Bible To Children*. Nashville, TN: Abingdon, 1997.

- Arts, Crafts, Inventions
- Body Language
- Creative Movement, Dance, Sign Language
- Drama, Motions, Pantomime, Puppets, Role Play
- Exercises, Physical Activities, Sports

Interpersonal/Relational Intelligence

Interpersonal/Relational Intelligence is the ability to perceive and make distinctions in the feelings, moods, intentions, and motivation of other people. It includes sensitivity to facial expressions, gestures, and voice. Motivation and learning in Interpersonal/Relational Intelligence stems from bouncing ideas off others and from cooperative learning tasks. Learners in this style prefer to work with others on a project or shared study.

Cooperative, group, paired, or team learning helps this student flourish. These types of learners are stifled by introspection and long periods of silent study. Methods most preferred in teaching learners of this style are:

- Answering questions
- Brainstorming ideas
- Comparing and contrasting ideas
- Cooperative learning, Group projects, Team activities
- Interviews, Dialogue, Discussion
- Playing cooperative games

Intrapersonal/Introspective Intelligence

Intrapersonal/Introspective Intelligence is the ability to act adaptively on the basis of self-knowledge and a capacity for self-understanding. Being aware of one's dreams, feelings, inner moods, intentions, intuition, motivations, and spirituality is part and parcel of the intelligence.

People with Intrapersonal/Introspective Intelligence learn best by working alone on projects. They will choose to reflect and be self-directed in their learning paths. Suggested methods in this style of learning are:

- Centering, Guided Imagery, Meditation
- Emotional processing
- Identifying with characters in a story
- Journaling
- Research projects
- Silent reflection, centering, and inward journey
- Thinking strategies
- Working alone

Logical/Mathematical Intelligence

Logical/Mathematical Intelligence is the capacity to use numbers effectively and to reason well. This includes sensitivity to logical patterns and relationships. Those with this learning style enjoy meeting a new challenge or problem solving.

People with Logical/Mathematical Intelligence are apt to categorize and classify things. They are skilled at deductive and inductive reasoning processes. Rational thinking is the primary tool they use in learning. Individuals that favor Logical/Mathematical Intelligence find it difficult to function in arenas of confusion or chaos, too much repetition, and unspecified goals.

Suggested methods for this learning style include:

- Codes, Games
- Experiments
- Exploring patterns and relationships

- Field trips
- Graphic organizers
- Number and word puzzles
- Problem solving and sequencing

Musical/Rhythmic Intelligence

Musical/Rhythmic Intelligence is the capacity to perceive, discriminate, transform, and express musical forms. People with Musical/Rhythmic Intelligence learn using rhythm, melody, and music combined with the information to be learned. They enjoy being surrounded by sound and rhythm and understand these as learning tools. Long reading or writing assignments, lectures, and large amounts of seat work bores and causes stress to this type of learner. Suggested learning methods are:

- Bible verses set to music
- Experiencing nature sounds
- Humming, singing, and listening to music
- Learning hymns and musicals
- Listening to and learning story songs
- Making and playing instruments
- Writing new words to familiar tunes
- Writing or performing musical compositions

Naturalist Intelligence

Naturalist Intelligence is the capacity to appreciate, enjoy, and understand the natural world, especially the ability to nurture animals and plants and to observe and organize patterns in the natural environment.

People who exhibit strength in the naturalist intelligence are very much at home in nature. They enjoy being outdoors, camping, and hiking, as well as studying and learning about animals and plants. They can easily classify and identify various species.

Methods to use to teach those who prefer this style include:

- Collecting and classifying nature items
- Field trips to natural history museums, nature centers, and zoos
- Hands-on labs
- Outdoor activities

Verbal/Linguistic Intelligence

Verbal/Linguistic Intelligence is the capacity to use words effectively, either orally or in writing. People with Verbal/Linguistic Intelligence learn by saying things aloud, hearing words spoken, and seeing words in print. They employ memory and recall and become frustrated with verbal stimulation and challenging concepts.

Methods preferred by this type of learner are:

- Books and Tapes
- Completing sentences
- Debate
- Memorizing dates, names, and trivia
- Reading and telling stories
- Writing litanies, poems, and stories

Visual/Spatial Intelligence

Visual/Spatial Intelligence is the ability to perceive the visual-spatial world accurately and to perform transformations upon those perceptions. It includes the capacity to visualize, to graphically represent visual or spatial ideas.

People with Visual/Spatial Intelligence learn by visualizing and dreaming about concepts and ideas. They incorporate sight as well as mental images. "Visuals" enhance their learning. On the other hand, too much printed material and writing will frustrate and discourage those who learn in this style.

Preferred methods in this learning style are:
- Art activities in various media
- Designing and building models
- Drawing, painting, and sculpting
- Graphs, maps, pictures, and puzzles
- Pretending, guided imagery, and visualization
- Studying symbols and using charts and posters
- Video

Using the Resource

Perhaps you have some questions about how to use this resource. Let's consider a few ways that this book will be helpful to anyone from the volunteer catechist leading a religion lesson in a parish setting to the professional educator adapting this information for use in a parochial school classroom.

Maybe you are one of those catechists who work from a prescribed curriculum or textbook to teach a class. The instructions are clear about what lessons to teach and the basic information that you need to convey, but you are looking for a way to make the class more meaningful as well as more memorable, so you enhance it with a monthly theme, be it based around a season of the year, a moral lesson, or a historical figure.

This resource takes up that idea and offers a monthly theme appropriate for any classroom setting based on the life of a saint. Your assignment every March, for example, might be to teach the story of Saint Patrick, whose feast day is on March 17. Knowing the group you work with, you want to enhance the basic theme which focuses mostly upon comprehension of biographical information. You want to involve the learners in the story so that they will appreciate the thrill and challenge of God's plan for Patrick's life, as well as appreciate God's plan for their lives. That's the point at which *Many Saints, Many Ways* becomes an extremely helpful resource.

Using this resource in March, then, you would review the eight techniques presented on Saint Patrick. From the options, you would choose one or more learning styles that would be most helpful. For example, to give the students the most information about Patrick, you might choose a first-person story retelling of his life. To help them to experience and attach personal meaning to Patrick's spirituality, using gestures to accompany a song based on his "Peace Prayer" would be appropriate. To explore the church's teaching on the Trinity, you might select Patrick's explanation of the shamrock and have the learners make a triptych. Depending upon your situation, you could "layer" the learning by using one technique a week; or, if time was limited, you could prepare a single lesson with one or more activities to reinforce the learning. The activities offered can be used to open, enrich, expand, or conclude any lesson.

Let's consider another situation. You may be a religious educator who is free to select the story you wish to tell based on the calendar of saints or the emphasis of a particular program. However, just knowing the focus of a lesson is not enough. Effective teachers know that a lesson has key elements that guide student learning from the introduction of an objective to a meaningful outcome. They accept responsibility for planning each lesson, much like an accomplished cook plans a balanced menu from appetizer to dessert.

You decide, for instance, that you want to focus a fall "back-to-school" lesson around the life of Saint Hildegard of Bingen, whose feast day is commemorated on September 17. Knowing your group, you decide that you want to use an interactive approach to convey the importance of offering our gifts to God. This book can help you plan each key element of a successful lesson. You want to find something "catchy" to help introduce the lesson and the objective. So you sift through the eight activities contained in the September chapter and select a game as the opener. Deciding that you first want to introduce Hildegard and her background, you choose to begin with the "Logical/Mathematical" approach of the matching game. Next, to convey Hildegard's emphasis on a life of prayer, you select the "Intrapersonal" activity of creating a prayer candle. However, if your group requires a more active approach, you could select the "Naturalist" project and have them create puppets to express Hildegard's concern and care for the environment. Finally, you want to tie learning about Hildegard's gifts to an invitation to the students to offer their own talents to God. You choose the "Bodily/Kinesthetic" suggestion as a closing activity, using the writings of Hildegard to inspire students to think about God's role in their own lives.

Alternately, the course of study in your religious education curriculum may call for study of saints or their related themes at various times of the year other than around saints' feast days. The lessons for a particular saint are not explicitly tied to the month of a feast day. You can use any of the lessons at any time of the year based on focus on a saint or on emphasis of one or more of the multiple intelligences.

Two main values of this book, then, are that lessons on saints can be refreshed on a monthly and yearly basis and that students who learn in different ways will have plenty of opportunities to learn in the style that *best* fits their intelligence. Jesus used "Multiple Intelligences" before it was educational theory. Jesus improvised the lesson based on his listeners and their needs. While none of us can expect to teach like the Master, we can adopt a more flexible approach that allows creativity and innovation to guide our lesson preparation and presentation.

While the activities in *Many Saints, Many Ways* are mainly intended for students in grades 1 to 6 they may be easily adapted for use with adolescents or young adults, either in large or small group settings.

So although the stories of the saints have been told, re-told, written about, and re-written countless times, *Many Saints, Many Ways* offers participants an opportunity to explore and experience the message anew. As you use this resource, may you find many ways to share Biblical stories, historical stories, and your own personal stories in order to keep alive the purpose of every saint: to draw each of us closer to God.

JANUARY
SAINT AGNES

Biography of Saint Agnes

Little is known for certain about Saint Agnes of Rome because she lived such a long time ago and she was so young when she died. Some information about Agnes was recorded by Saint Ambrose, Pope Damasus, and Prudentius. Scholars believe that Agnes was born on January 28, 291 A.D. in Rome to an influential family.

At an early age Agnes made a confession of faith, probably with her parents permission; otherwise, she would have been betrothed to a man of her father's choosing. Instead, she promised herself to Christ and refused all offers of marriage, announcing that she was "promised to the Lord of the Universe" who would always love her and never forsake her.

Early historians write that one of her rejected suitors, a well-to-do Roman, accused her of being a Christian and reported her to the authorities. Since it was illegal to worship any God other than the Roman pagan gods, Agnes was arrested and threatened with punishment, even torture. Some accounts record that she was to be publicly humiliated and her virtue ruined, but God protected Agnes and no harm befell her. Still trying to persuade her to renounce her Christian faith, the judge ordered that she be executed.

Instead of intimidating the twelve-year-old, the threat filled her with resolve. She welcomed death as the entrance to eternity. Agnes is reported to have gone to her death like a bride to a wedding. Some write that her executioners first tried to burn her, but the flames failed. She was then killed by the sword in 304 A.D., during the persecutions of the Emperor Diocletian. Regardless of conflicting stories of how she was killed, all authorities agree on one thing: Agnes, the courageous and faithful young virgin, went happily to meet Jesus, whom she loved more than life itself. Saint Agnes' feast day is observed on January 21.

Mission of Saint Agnes

Saint Agnes of Rome did not seek a mission for God. Instead, God's mission found her. At a time when Christians were being persecuted, Agnes had the depth of faith and commitment to remain true to her calling in Christ. She did not fear when powerful authorities attempted to get her to renounce her beliefs. She used her trials as an opportunity to witness to God's love and faithful care. By facing her torture and death with Christ's unwavering peace, her martyrdom turned the hearts of the Romans who saw her slain for her faith.

Legacy of Saint Agnes

The life and death of Saint Agnes leave an important legacy for us today. Her youthful innocence and determined faith proved to those who witnessed her martyrdom that Christianity offered more than their superstitions and traditions. Agnes' sacrifice helped open the door for the common acceptance of Christianity. On a personal level, Saint Agnes shows us the importance of all of God's faithful followers, no matter what age. Her name means "lamb" in Latin, reminding Christians of the value found in a life of purity and sacrifice. It is a tradition on her feast day for two lambs to be brought to her Basilica in Rome and blessed. Later, their wool is shorn and woven into palliums for the pope to give to the archbishops. These leaders of the church wear the stoles as reminders that they are called to shepherd Christ's flock.

Bodily/Kinesthetic Intelligence

Learn

By searching through resource materials, creating stories to relate, and reinforcing speech with body language, participants will discover information about Saint Agnes and learn to determine facts about her life.

Locate

Markers; Paper; Pencils or pens; Poster board; Resource materials on Saint Agnes

Advance Preparation

Prepare a set of posters, one with the word "Truth" and the other with the word "Fable" for each group.

Lead

When learning about saints from the earliest days of the church, researchers must read carefully and compare the information found in varied sources. One begins to determine what seems more reliable by seeing which information is consistently reported and by determining which sources seem most credible. Some stories must be taken "with a grain of salt" because there is little to confirm or substantiate their claims. This is very true regarding the life of Saint Agnes of Rome.

Because there are so many legends and stories that have grown up around the life of Saint Agnes, encourage the students to research and review as many sources as possible concerning her life. Because some of the stories concern sensitive issues like the threat to Agnes' virginity, preview the sources that are to be used and screen them for age-appropriate language and suitable treatment of the information.

Explain to the participants that they are going to play a game called "Truth or Fable." Divide the group into two or more teams, and give them different biographical resources to explore about Saint Agnes. Tell them that they must be prepared to tell at least as many stories as there are teams. If there are two teams, each must prepare two stories; if there are four groups, each must prepare four stories, and so on. They should at least have one story that they have judged to be the complete truth and one that they think is an exaggeration; or they may make up a completely imaginary story to try to trick the other team(s) into accepting it as the truth.

For example, a group could tell the true story of the burial of Saint Agnes, explaining that her tomb was located on the Via Nomentana in Rome in a catacomb eventually named for her. This site later became the location for the Basilica of Saint Agnes built by the daughter of the Emperor Constantine, Constantina. The object would be to include numerous details that would challenge the other teams' ability to recognize the story as completely true or not. Of course, the storytellers could also be creative and narrate a potentially believable, but completely inaccurate, story. For example, they could claim that Agnes, before she was martyred, was condemned to prison. While in jail, Agnes ministered to the other prisoners unbeknownst to her jailers. Today she is the patron saint of jailers.

Once the teams have prepared their stories, the groups then take turns telling their tales. Storytellers should be animated, using their body language to communicate non-verbally the account they want to share. The others listen, and each group decides what they think of the story, holding up a placard with Truth or Fable to cast their vote. The speakers then reveal the correct answer. The teams earn a point each time they correctly identify whether the tale is "Truth" or "Fable." Play until all stories have been told or until one team is definitely the winner. Discuss the importance of researching to find the truth and being responsible reporters of what we learn.

Interpersonal Intelligence

Learn

By playing a game of "Jeopardy," participants will learn information about the life of Saint Agnes.

Locate

Chalk or markers; Chalkboard, construction paper, or poster board; Index cards; Pencils or pens; Resource material on Saint Agnes; Tacks or tape; Timer.

Lead

The word "jeopardy" means "risk" which clearly relates to the story of Saint Agnes of Rome, who risked all—including her life—for her faith in Christ. The interactive format of the game "Jeopardy" is a good method to use to teach lessons related to the accounts about this popular saint.

Review information about Saint Agnes by playing a game like that of the television game show Jeopardy. In the game of Jeopardy the answer is revealed and the question must be supplied. To prepare a Jeopardy game board, select five categories, such as Facts, History, People, Symbols, and Vocabulary. Mark five columns on a piece of poster board—one for each classification. Write five questions for each category on separate index cards and indicate the point value on the back of each card—10, 20, 30, 40, and 50. If possible, use different color index cards for each of the five categories. Sample questions could include:

Facts
Answer: Most Scholars believe that Saint Agnes was martyred at this age.
Question: What is the age of twelve or thirteen?

History
Answer: This ancient city was the site of Saint Agnes' martyrdom.
Question: What is Rome?

People
Answer: This person reported to the authorities that Agnes was a Christian.
Question: Who is her rejected suitor?

Symbols
Answer: In paintings of her martyrdom, this instrument of death is often seen lying at the feet of Agnes.
Question: What is a sword?

Vocabulary
Answer: This word is used to name those who die for the cause of Christ.
Question: What is a martyr?

Once the questions are compiled, attach the index cards for each category in a vertical column under the corresponding heading. Be sure that the point value, rather than the answer, is displayed.

Inform the players that one answer at a time will be selected and revealed. The first individual or team will have one minute to state the question. If they provide the correct question, they will be given the point value indicated on the card. If they cannot come up with the question, the other player or team will have a turn to attempt to answer it. Rotate teams after each question. The game ends when all questions are answered or when a predetermined number of points are reached.

Intrapersonal Intelligence

Learn

By participating in an essay contest related to the values of Saint Agnes, students will affirm their personal commitment to follow God.

Locate

Awards; Essay guidelines; Paper; Pens; Resource materials on Saint Agnes.

Advance Preparation

Form essay contest committee, prepare guidelines, and secure judges.

Lead

Saint Agnes was able to lay down her life for her beliefs because of her inner convictions. Despite the dangers she faced, Agnes was unwilling to renounce her faith in Jesus Christ. Having strong inner convictions is important for all of God's followers, whether young or old. One way to discover and solidify our values is to put them in writing. The word "essay" literally means "to try" or "to attempt," suggesting that we try to find the words to say exactly what we think and feel on a given topic.

Involve the students in a writing activity focused on a theme such as "Even the Young Can Serve God." In preparation, explain that Agnes is one of the most popular saints even though she lived and died so long ago. Discuss reasons for her popularity, suggesting that perhaps people are surprised when the young have such strong faith and beliefs. Ask the participants if they think that today's youth also have a firm commitment to follow God. Challenge the students to consider their own willingness to serve God in today's world. Have them reflect on the ways that they already serve God or the ways that they would like to serve God in the future. Distribute paper and pencils or pens and ask the students to write a few sentences that explore their inner thoughts and feelings about serving God. Invite them to revise their entries into an essay to be shared with others. Offer an essay contest for those who wish to participate.

Distribute guidelines for the essay activity, which contain information such as:

Age Categories

List ages or grades of those who may enter the essay contest.

Awards

Offer a prize, perhaps a button or a certificate, to everyone who enters. List the first, second, and third place prizes. These could be books, gift certificates, or T-shirts. Note any other type of recognition, such as reading the winning essays at a public function or awarding something special to the classroom submitting the most entries.

Contact Persons

List names and telephone numbers of people who may be called for information or questions.

Deadline

Include date and time by which all essays must be submitted.

Format

State how entries are to be submitted, for example, handwritten or typed on one side of an 8 1/2" x 11" paper. Indicate the length of the essay, such as 250 to 500 words. Note that name, grade, parish, or school, and phone are to be printed on the back of the page.

Judging

Indicate the criteria upon which the entries will be judged, such as content, imagination, neatness, style and so forth. Name categories of judges like librarians, pastors, and teachers. Give specific names, if possible.

Other Information

Note whether the entries will become the property of the sponsoring group(s) or be returned to the writer. Indicate that the decision of the judges is final.

Sponsors

List the name(s) of the sponsoring group(s).

Submissions

Provide the name of the person or place and the address to which the entries must be delivered or mailed by the deadline.

Theme

Pick an open-ended theme around which entries can be based, for example, "Commitment to God means . . . " or "Even the Young Can Serve God . . . ".

When the essays are completed, make arrangements to have some of the participants read their written work in the classroom, the parish, or the school. Other options include mounting the essays and displaying them in public locations, submitting a sampling of entries to a publication such as a church bulletin or a school newsletter, or compiling an anthology of pieces and making them available to others. As a creative exchange, send the essays to children in other parishes and schools and invite them to send their ideas back to the originating group.

Logical/Mathematical Intelligence

Learn

By creating a dictionary of vocabulary words, students will become familiar with terms associated with the lives of the saints.

Locate

Bible Dictionaries; Dictionaries; Hole punches; Resource information on Saint Agnes and other saints; Markers; Paper; Pencils or pens; Ribbon, string, or yarn; Scissors.

Lead

While the stories of the saints vary remarkably, there are some words that remain consistent in the celebration and the commemoration of the lives of these people of faith. These terms are often heard and repeated without taking time to make sure that everyone understands their definitions and connotations. When referring to the saints, we use many words that may need further explanation for children as well as adults—those new to the faith as well as those mature in their beliefs.

As a class project, or an individual or small group activity, create dictionaries—lists of vocabulary words and their explanations—as a way to define, or interpret, some of the terms connected with the study of the saints, and specifically Saint Agnes of Rome in January. Begin by brainstorming a list or by looking through resource materials to find key words and unfamiliar terms that need to be explained. Try to include terms like *feast day, martyr, persecution, saint,* and *symbol* as well as words such as *canonization, patron saint, relic, sacred* and *testimony.*

Work individually or in small groups to locate definitions in standard dictionaries and in reference books. Provide paper and pencils or pens and instruct the students to create a "dictionary" by listing the selected words in alphabetical order and writing a phrase or a sentence to explain each of them. Offer examples, such as:

Canonization: A formal sanction of the church recognizing a person as a saint.

Emblem: A visible symbol that represents the life and teachings of a saint.

Feast Day: A day set aside to commemorate the life of the saint, generally on the anniversary of the saint's death.

Martyr: Those who have died for their faith because they love God more than they love life.

Patron Saint: A specific saint who serves as a guardian of a particular person, place, or institution.

Persecution: The infliction of distress upon a person because of his or her beliefs.

Relic: The bodily remains of a saint or of an object associated with a saint, reverenced as a memorial.

Saint: A holy person who makes it easier for others to believe in God because of the example of his or her faith and life.

Once the list is compiled, provide materials so that each person or group may add a cover. Decorate the sheet with markers and add a title, if desired. Punch the pages and bind them with ribbon, string, or yarn. Share the dictionaries so that others may gain a better understanding of these important words from the lives of the saints as well as grasp the meaning of God's great love for each of God's children.

Musical/Rhythmic Intelligence

Learn

By learning the story of the hymn "Jesus Loves Me" and by making a fingerprint heart, participants will affirm the message that gave Saint Agnes the courage to live her faith.

Locate

Construction paper; Markers; Music for "Jesus Loves Me" (Children's Hymn Book); Pattern for heart; Scissors; Stamp pads; Wet paper towels.

Lead

The strength that Saint Agnes displayed as a child came directly from her relationship with Christ. She was able to face the sacrifice she had to make in order to remain faithful to Jesus because she understood the sacrifice that Jesus had made for her. No matter how difficult life's challenges are, we can overcome them if we remember the single most important truth: Jesus loves us, each of us, individually. When the love of Jesus is imprinted in our hearts, we can leave our mark on life, too, just as Saint Agnes did.

Sing the song "Jesus Loves Me" as a celebration of this great message of the Christian faith. Then teach the participants the story behind the familiar hymn and invite them to affirm the message by making thumbprint hearts.

Begin by reviewing the words of the song, "Jesus Loves Me," and singing the hymn as a class.

Verse One
"Jesus loves me! This I know,
For the Bible tells me so;
Little ones to him belong,
They are weak but he is strong.

Chorus
Yes, Jesus loves me!
Yes, Jesus loves me!
Yes, Jesus loves me!
The Bible tells me so.

Verse Two
Jesus loves me! He who died
Heaven's gates to open wide;
He will wash away my sin,
Let his little child come in.

Verse Three
Jesus loves me! He will stay
Close beside me all the way;
He's prepared a home for me,
And some day his face I'll see.

Before sharing the story of the hymn, make a sample teaching tool. Fold a piece of construction paper in half. Draw half of a heart on one side of the paper, making sure that the left side of the shape touches the fold of the sheet. Cut out the symbol and unfold. Using a washable ink stamp pad, place the thumb on the pad and then make a print in the center of the front of the heart. Form a cross shape by adding fingerprints around the four sides of the center impression as the tale is told. Write the words "Jesus Loves Me" on the outside of the paper.

"Jesus Loves Me" Story Suggestion

(Hold up the heart shape.) What does the heart shape symbolize? (Someone should say "Love.") If you were going to think of someone who loves you, you might think of your parents or grandparents, or sisters or brothers. But in the church, Jesus shows us God's love best of all. Jesus came as a human being to show us God's love.

There is something special about being a human being, something that distinguishes each one of us. And that is a fingerprint. So to remind ourselves that Jesus was a person who came to earth to show us God's love, let's make a fingerprint stamp right here in the middle of this heart, okay? (Make the first fingerprint.)

Isn't that neat? Do you know that each and every person has a different fingerprint? No one else's fingerprint is exactly like yours. God made each one of us unique. And Jesus loves each one of us, just as we are. Let's stamp a second fingerprint right above the first one to remind us that each of us is loved by Jesus. (Make the second fingerprint.)

That really is the heart of the Christian message—Jesus loves me. There is a song called "Jesus Loves Me." The song was first a poem in a story written by Anna Warner together with her sister Susan Warner. They both became famous authors in the middle 1800s. "Jesus Loves Me" was a poem spoken to a sick child in their book *Say and Seal*. The sisters had been left penniless when their parents died, but they were people of strong faith. They taught Sunday school classes to young cadets at West Point Academy and used their unique gifts of writing to share the message of Jesus' love. They were both loved by their students and were even given full military honors at their funerals. To remember Anna and Susan Warner, let's put two more fingerprints on our heart, one on each side of our first two stamps. (Add two fingerprints to the design.) Is this starting to remind you of something? It looks like a cross, doesn't it?

We just need to add one more stamp to our heart. This stamp completes our design, and it reminds us that the poem "Jesus Loves Me" became complete when a man named William Bradbury set the words to music and added the chorus "Yes, Jesus loves me. The Bible tells me so." With his contribution, the song "Jesus Loves Me" became an immediate success. It has since become one of the most famous hymns sung all around the world. It is often the first song sung by missionaries to new Christians. A professor very knowledgeable about the Bible always reminded his students that the greatest truth in the Christian faith could be summed up in the words: "Jesus loves me; this I know."

A famous saint we remember in January, on January 21 to be specific, lived this truth. Saint Agnes of Rome was just twelve or thirteen years old when she was put to death for her commitment to Christ. She was able to face the sacrifice she had to make in order to remain faithful to Jesus because she understood the sacrifice that Jesus had made for her. No matter how difficult life's challenges are, we can overcome them if we remember the single most important truth: Jesus loves us, each of us, individually. When the love of Jesus is imprinted in our hearts, we can leave our mark on life, too, just as Saint Agnes did.

Once the story is shared, provide supplies and guide the group as they create fingerprint hearts. Share the message that "Jesus Loves Me" by having the participants write a message on the inside of the heart shape and giving the completed greetings to others.

Naturalist Intelligence

Learn

By making and decorating a stole, participants will recall the symbolism of Saint Agnes' name and the tradition of making palliums for archbishops.

Locate

Bible(s); Cardboard or card stock; Fabric glue; Felt, white; Felt scraps; Newspaper or shelf paper; Pattern for sheep (one size or various sizes); Pattern for stole; Pencils; Permanent markers; Pins; Scissors; Trims (buttons, rickrack, sequins); Wool pieces.

Advance Preparation

Obtain measurements for the stole(s) for the pastor(s). Prepare a stole pattern by cutting an eighteen-inch by thirty-six inch piece from newspaper or shelf paper. Adjust the pattern paper so the stole will reach to the waist, knee, or other desired length.

Lead

In the Greek language the name "Agnes" means "pure." In Latin, however, it sounds like the word *Agnus,* which means lamb. It is also associated with the term *Agnus Dei,* or "Lamb of God." Because of this correlation, Saint Agnes' emblem in art is often depicted as a lamb. From this connection comes a tradition celebrated each year in Rome. On Saint Agnes' feast day, January 21, two lambs are brought to Saint Agnes' Basilica for blessing during the festal mass. The nuns in a cloister then raise them. During Holy Week, before Easter, the wool of these two sheep is sheared and woven into palliums—special stoles. The pope confers these woven white wool stoles on archbishops in various jurisdictions to wear on their shoulders as a reminder that they are the shepherds of Christ's flock. The position of the stole is a reminder of the sheep borne on the shoulder of the Good Shepherd, Jesus.

Share information about Saint Agnes' name and the tradition of the lambs with the students. Then invite them to create a stole with symbols of sheep to give as a gift to the pastor of the parish or school "flock." It may be necessary to create several stoles depending on the number of priests to whom they will be given. In advance, or with the participants, cut a stole for each recipient. Place the stole pattern on the white felt and pin it down. Cut out the fabric.

Provide sheep patterns, pencils, felt in white and other colors, and scissors. Assist each pupil as he or she traces a lamb on the felt and cuts it out. Offer fabric glue as well as permanent markers and trims, such as buttons or sequins for eyes, rickrack to outline the shape, and wool tufts to add a three-dimensional effect. Guide the learners as they personalize their sheep.

Place the stole on a table and help each child arrange sheep in a random pattern or in a symmetrical design. Avoid too many sheep around the neck area to allow for smoother draping. Glue the pieces in place.

Present the gift to the pastor and share the story of Saint Agnes, an innocent young lamb who served the Great Shepherd with her life.

Verbal/Linguistic Intelligence

Learn

By experiencing a first-person narrative, participants will comprehend biographical information regarding Saint Agnes and connect the events of her life to a related story from scripture (1 Samuel 16:1-13) and to their commitment to God.

Locate

Bible; Costume for "Father" Storyteller; Story script.

Lead

Share the story of Saint Agnes and tell the related Bible story as a first-person narrative. To enhance learning and to make the story memorable, a costumed character representing Agnes' "father" should relate memories about his favorite daughter and saint, Agnes.

"Father" Story Script
(adapted from 1 Samuel 16:1-13)

Hello, welcome in the name of the Lord. We follow Jesus in this household, and it is his name we revere. Our daughter taught us that. Perhaps you have heard of her—Agnes, our dear little lamb. She was beautiful to look at, but even more beautiful to know.

Most fathers would have been busy sorting through all of the best bachelors to make a good match for such a remarkable daughter. And I would have too, if she had permitted me. She could have had whomever she desired. Well, as a matter of fact, she did. Agnes' desire was to be a bride of Christ, to dedicate herself to live in the service of God. Her mother and I accepted her choice even though it put her in grave danger. We couldn't see what God had in mind.

Our story reminds me of another father whose story is found in the Old Testament of the Bible. He had trouble recognizing that his child was chosen by God, too. Jesse, the father of David, brought all of his older sons to Samuel when the prophet was looking for Israel's new king. It didn't even occur to Jesse to bring his youngest son, David, before the prophet. David was too young for God to use. When Samuel insisted, David was sent for, and the old prophet recognized that this youth was chosen by God for a special purpose. Through David's family, God brought forth his Messiah, Jesus, the One whose sacrifice assures us all of eternal life.

It was this promise of eternal life in Christ that gave Agnes the strength for her life. Like Jesse, I did not recognize at first that God's hand was upon her. Once Agnes began to receive proposals of marriage, I worried for her. She tried to laughingly reject advances by saying she was promised to the Lord of the Universe because he would always love her and never betray her. But such answers were finally not enough. When she rejected one young man's proposal of marriage, he turned her in as a suspected Christian.

Agnes accepted her fate. She refused to renounce Christ. Our hearts broke to realize that our daughter would die before she ever became a woman. Yet we were amazed at her faith and courage in the face of death, and we were filled with admiration. The week after Agnes died for her faith, her mother and I went to her tomb, grieving because it would have been her birthday. But God granted us a vision of our daughter alive in eternity and surrounded by light. Like Jesse, I have come to know that as an earthly father, I look on outward appearance and see only flesh and blood. But God our heavenly Father looks on the heart and sees great possibilities.

Visual/Spatial Intelligence

Learn

By exploring visual art depicting Saint Agnes of Rome, participants will come to appreciate the many expressions of her life that artists have portrayed over the years.

Locate

Resource materials containing art depicting Saint Agnes of Rome.

Lead

Throughout history, the lives of the saints have long been preserved and celebrated through the visual arts. This is especially true for the life of Saint Agnes of Rome. She is represented in various media including icons, paintings, sculpture, and stained glass. In art, Agnes is generally pictured as a young maiden with long hair. Sometimes she is also shown with a sword at her throat; naked, covered by an angel or by her long hair; crowned and holding a scroll; with a lamb—*Agnus*—as a symbol of her purity and sacrifice; with a palm as the emblem of a martyr; and with a dove having a ring in its beak.

Take a field trip or a "virtual" tour of the representations of Saint Agnes available in a variety of places. Visit locations in person, in books, or on the World Wide Web. Find as many different depictions of Agnes' life and legacy as possible. Then create a display of drawings, illustrations, and photos on a bulletin board, wall, or tabletop. Begin a search with some of the following possibilities:

In Class

- Discover drawings in prayer books.
- Examine pictures in resource materials about saints.
- Find information in encyclopedias.
- Look in art books for paintings related to the life of Saint Agnes.
- Page through books on periods of art such as the Middle Ages or the Italian Renaissance to find illustrations of Saint Agnes.
- Search the Internet for biographical and historical sites using keywords such as Saint Agnes, Images of Saint Agnes or Relics of Saint Agnes.
- Visit Websites for world-renowned museums such as The Hermitage in Saint Petersburg, Russia; the Louvre in Paris, France; the Metropolitan Museum of Art in New York; or the National Gallery of Art in Washington, D.C. to search for representations of Saint Agnes in their collections.
- Watch a film or video about the saints that includes Saint Agnes.

Out of Class

- Browse a religious goods store and look at items such as books, commemorative plates, note cards, postcards, posters and prayer cards.
- Tour a church named for Saint Agnes and look at items like icons, medallions, mosaics, paintings, sculpture, stained glass, and tapestries.
- Visit an art museum and view the collection of sacred pieces, looking for representations of Saint Agnes.

FEBRUARY
SAINT SCHOLASTICA

Biography of Saint Scholastica

Saint Scholastica was a twin, born with her brother Benedict in Norcia, Italy, about 480 A D to parents of the Roman nobility. Scholastica's father and mother dedicated her to God in her infancy. She and her brother were devoted to each other, and when Benedict decided to become a monk, Scholastica became a nun. Benedict founded an important monastery at Monte Cassino, establishing what became known as the "Benedictine Rule." The monks who lived there taught people how to treat each other with gentleness and respect.

Scholastica decided that she would be the first woman to live under the Benedictine rule. Just five miles south of her brother's monastery, Scholastica established a convent at Plombariola where she served as the abbess. From that time on, Scholastica only saw her brother once a year since most of their lives were devoted to religious matters. They would meet at a little house about halfway between the convent and the abbey. When together, the siblings would talk about God and pray together over spiritual matters. At the end of their day's visit, each would return to their cloistered lives. Once, at what turned out to be the last of these yearly meetings, Scholastica begged her brother to remain until the next day. He refused because his rules forbid him to spend the night outside of the monastery. When he would not relent, Scholastica started to weep and pray. A great rainstorm began to accompany her tears, a storm so furious that neither Saint Benedict nor his companions could depart. Consequently, the brother and sister stayed up talking and sharing spiritual joys the entire night.

When Scholastica said goodbye to her brother the next morning, it was to be their final parting. Three days later, Scholastica died. Benedict, back in his monastery, beheld a vision of Scholastica's soul in the form of a dove as it ascended into heaven. Benedict had some of his brothers bring Scholastica's body to the monastery, and he placed it in the tomb that he had prepared for himself. Scholastica died in the year 543 A D. Saint Benedict followed her soon after and was buried with his sister in the same grave. Saint Scholastica's feast day is observed on February 10.

Mission of Saint Scholastica

Little is known about Scholastica's actual mission in life. What is commonly accepted comes from the six paragraphs written about fifty years after her death in *Saint Gregory the Great's Dialogues.* However, it is clear that Saint Scholastica lived a life of devotion to God. Her brother was certainly a strong influence on her life, but she determined for herself to accept the rule that he had established for his monks. Her example of dedication and commitment served as an inspiration to him, as well. Scholastica demonstrated the power of a life devoted to prayer and obedience to God. Her determination and discipline helped establish a religious order that sought to bring others to trust in God and to treat one another with gentle respect.

Legacy of Saint Scholastica

The one great story of Scholastica's life is of her final meeting with Benedict. Whether she knew that this would be their last time together is not certain, but she clearly could not bear to see their yearly meeting come to an end. While Benedict refused his dear sister's request because of the rule of his order, Scholastica understood that sometimes people are more important than rules. She went "over his head" directly to God. Her fervent prayers and tears brought an intervening rainstorm that kept her beloved brother with her for a few more hours. The legacy of Saint Scholastica is that, while discipline is key to developing a spiritual life, devotion to God is more than being bound by rules. Loving God is also about loving one another. And when we trust in a loving God, we can ask for what we want, for God knows when it is good to say "Yes" to our requests.

Bodily/Kinesthetic Intelligence

Learn

By answering questions in a relay race, participants will enjoy reviewing information about the life of Saint Scholastica.

Locate

Chairs; Duplicating equipment; Envelopes; Questions about Saint Scholastica; Scissors.

Advance Preparation

Prepare a set of questions about the life of Saint Scholastica. Twelve sample questions have been provided, however, if additional questions are needed, or if questions with varying degrees of difficulty are desired, use additional resource material to prepare your own.

Make two copies of the questions, cut them apart, and place each set in a separate envelope. Set each envelope on the chair at the midpoint of each "race course."

Lead

Growing up together, the twins, Benedict and Scholastica, shared an uncommon devotion to God and to one another. Although each made a commitment to enter the cloistered life, they must have looked forward to their annual day-long visit as a time to celebrate their devotion to God and their relationship with each other. Every year Benedict and Scholastica would meet halfway between the monastery and the convent to share their spiritual insights and to spend time in prayer. Their loving communion united them as brother and sister in the faith as they were already in life.

Scholastica and Benedict must have shared a special connection that transcended ordinary sister and brother ties. To help the participants remember the story of these special twins, have the students run a unique kind of relay race as partners, or "twins." Establish two race courses with start and finish lines. They should go from a beginning point to a midpoint, such as a chair, and back to the starting place. Once the courses are designed, organize the class into two groups and have each team line up as partners behind each start line. Station a coach at each midpoint.

Review the rules for the relay. Each pair will run to the midpoint and select a question from the envelope on the chair. One person will read the question, and the other will attempt to answer it. If the answer is correct, the coach will award a point. If the answer is incorrect, no point will be recorded. Then the partners run back to the start line to pass a "go" signal, such as a "tag," to the next players on the team who repeat the process. Generally, the first team to have all of its players finish the course or the group with the highest score is the winner.

Once the game is completed, remind the participants that the relay race can help them remember the energy that comes to those who work together to accomplish a goal, just like Scholastica and Benedict helped each other find the inspiration to serve God.

Sample Questions
1. Scholastica's brother's name was _____.
2. The twins grew up in their native land of _____.
3. The name of Benedict's monastery was _____.
4. Scholastica was the first woman to follow the Benedictine _____.
5. Scholastica and Benedict were _____.
6. Scholastica and Benedict met once each _____.
7. Scholastica kept Benedict from leaving by _____.
8. God answered Scholastica's prayer in the form of a _____.
9. After their last meeting, Scholastica lived only three _____.
10. When Scholastica died, Benedict saw her soul ascend to heaven in the form of a _____.
11. Benedict had Scholastica buried in his own _____.
12. When Benedict died he was buried with his twin _____.

Answers:
1. Benedict
2. Italy
3. Monte Cassino
4. Rule
5. twins
6. year
7. praying
8. thunderstorm
9. days
10. dove
11. grave
12. sister

Interpersonal Intelligence

Learn

By following Saint Scholastica's example of praying for others, participants will create a prayer prompter to use to remember the special people that God brings into their lives.

Locate

Construction paper; Duplicating equipment; Pattern for Prayer Prompter; Pens; Rulers; Scissors.

Advance Preparation

Cut construction paper into 4 1/2" x 12" pieces, one per person. Cut 2" x 4" pieces of construction paper, seven per person.

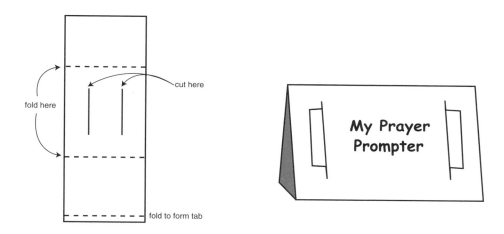

Lead

Within the Benedictine Order, life was lived in relationship. Saint Benedict's rule, whether at the monastery in Monte Cassino or the convent in Plombariola, was designed to help facilitate community, a commitment to living in harmony and mutual concern. At the center of this philosophy was devotion to a life of prayer. Benedict and Scholastica understood the importance of this kind of commitment because their own relationship was founded on the same principles. Their concern and love for one another found its expression in their mutual love for God. When they held their yearly meetings, the day was based on sharing spiritual insights and offering prayers to God. Ultimately, the lives of this brother and sister teach us the importance of grounding our human relationships in prayer. We must find the way to discipline ourselves to remember others, especially the special people that God brings into our lives—family and friends—in prayer.

Invite the group to make "Prayer Prompters" as a way to help them remember family and friends in their conversations with God. Show an example of a completed "Prayer Prompter" and demonstrate the process for constructing the teaching tool. Select one 4 1/2" x 12" piece of construction paper. Fold the long paper into thirds, with four inches in each section. Using the pattern provided, cut two vertical slits in the center section of the strip. The slits should be 2 1/2" long and 3" apart. Fold bottom edge of long piece back 3/8" to form tab. Glue the tab to the top edge to form triangle so that the prompter will stand on its own. Choose seven pieces of 2" x 4" paper. Using a pen, write one day of the week, Sunday through Saturday, up the left-hand side of each piece. Next, write the name of a family member or a friend on each slip. Insert the seven slips in order, with Sunday at the top, into the center section of the "Prayer Prompter."

Distribute supplies and guide the group as they construct their own "Prayer Prompters." Once the projects are completed, provide instructions for using the teaching tool. On Sunday, pray for the person whose name is written on the first slip. Then remove the piece and place it on the bottom of the "Prayer Prompter." On Monday, pray for the second person. Continue in this manner every day for the rest of the week. At the end of seven days, the first strip—Sunday—will be on top again. At this point, repeat the process or use new names and begin again.

Intrapersonal Intelligence

Learn

By creating a journal and recording spontaneous conversations with God, participants will be inspired to remember Saint Scholastica's example of turning to God in prayer in all circumstances of life.

Locate

Catalogs or magazines; Glue; Hole punch; Markers; 8 1/2" x 11" Construction paper, various colors (five or six sheets per person); Pens; Ribbon, string or yarn; Scissors; 8 1/2" x 11" White construction paper, two pieces per person.

Lead

Scholastica lived a life of prayer. Her devotion to God led her to choose the monastic life that embraced the discipline of regular prayer. To Scholastica, however, communion with God was not limited to specific hours or prescribed forms. She lived aware of the Divine Presence in each moment. Once, when her brother Benedict was ready to leave from their yearly visit in order to fulfill the rule of his order, she turned her request for him to stay to God, the One she knew was always listening. Saint Scholastica's example teaches us that prayer offers an occasion to bring God into every moment of every day. Spontaneous prayer offers the opportunity to pray about anything, anywhere, anytime. This type of silent or spoken prayer helps us recognize God in every part of life.

Explain that everyone will make a prayer scrapbook as a way to record the opportunities for spontaneous prayer that occur every day. Distribute two pieces of white construction paper and five or six sheets of colored paper to each student. Instruct them to make a book by placing the colored paper between the two pieces of white paper and folding the stack in half. Hole punch and tie the pages together with a length of ribbon, string, or yarn. Using markers, direct the students to letter the phrase "Prayer Scrapbook" on the front cover and to add decorations, if desired.

The Prayer Scrapbook may be completed in several ways. To finish the project in class, provide old magazines, scissors, glue and markers. Direct the group to print the words "Prayer Moment" on the pages of the scrapbook. Several headings describing these moments (including emotions, feelings, experiences) may be printed on the same page. Next, they should find pictures and words in the catalogs or magazines which depict their prayer moments, cut them out, and glue them to the pages. Illustrations may be drawn with markers, too.

To finish the project at home, direct the pupils to take the scrapbooks with them and to complete the pages as "prayer moments" occur or to record their thoughts at the end of each day. These moments may be portrayed with drawings, magazine photos, family photos, or actual objects. At a specified time, ask the students to bring the books to class to share their experiences with others.

Encourage the class to use the scrapbooks to remind them of the spontaneous opportunities for prayer every day.

Logical/Mathematical Intelligence

Learn

By constructing a ruler, participants will consider how God's rule is present in their own lives as it was for Saint Scholastica.

Locate

Markers; Pencils or pens; Poster board; Rulers; Scissors.

Lead

Scholastica decided that she would be ruled by the same discipline that her brother Benedict had instituted for the monastery, and subsequently the Order that he founded. Scholastica established the first Benedictine convent at Plombariola and so brought to women the religious rule that her brother had begun for men. Scholastica and her followers accepted the cloistered life and devoted themselves to prayer. Their commitment was to live a life ruled by God, to be people of peace, and to reflect the harmony of Christ's love.

Explain the history of Scholastica's commitment to live under Benedictine rule. Point out that both Benedict and Scholastica wanted their lives to be ruled by God and that their Order was designed to be a practical approach to living in harmony and peace on earth. Scholastica, as well as Benedict, knew that the amazing thing about God as our Ruler is that God rules our lives by invitation only. Certainly, God can control anything God chooses, but he chooses to give us freedom. We must decide who is to rule our lives—God or us. God wants to rule in our lives so that God's kingdom—God's plan or design for what is best for us—can become a reality on earth like it already is in heaven. Invite the participants to brainstorm guidelines for those who want God to rule their lives. Suggest verbs like *forgive, give, love, meditate, pray, share, study, trust, work,* and phrases like "be humble," "live in peace," "seek justice," "serve others," and "show mercy."

Make poster board rulers as a reminder that God ruled in Saint Scholastica's life. Offer rulers to use as a pattern, as well as poster board pieces, pencils and scissors. Tell each learner to trace a ruler onto a piece of poster board and to cut out the shape. Provide pens or markers and direct the group to add one-inch designations to the foot-long paper. In each square, tell them to write words associated with guidelines for letting God rule our lives. Refer to the brainstormed list for suggestions. Words may be printed horizontally or vertically in the spaces.

If desired, copy a quote on the back of the poster board piece, such as *Rule of Benedict* c. 72, "Let them prefer nothing whatever to Christ. And may he bring us all together to everlasting life!"

As an alternative to poster board pieces, provide a plastic or wooden ruler for each participant and complete the rest of the project using permanent marker to write words on the surface of the teaching tool.

Musical/Rhythmic Intelligence

Learn

By recreating the sounds of Saint Scholastica's experience of the rainstorm, participants will learn that God sometimes answers prayer in unexpected ways.

Locate

Cassette tape or CD of a rainstorm (Optional); Cassette or CD player (Optional).

Lead

Scholastica and Benedict were twins who each dedicated their lives to God. Benedict founded the Benedictine Order and Scholastica established a convent for women who would also follow her brother's established rule. Benedict's monastery at Monte Cassino was only about five miles from his sister's convent at Plombariola. Even though they lived close together, they only left the monastic life once a year to be together. Devoted to each other, they would spend the day sharing their love for God and praying together over spiritual matters. However, when the day ended, Benedict and his brothers were required by the rule of their order to return to the monastery. The final year of her life, Scholastica and Benedict met for the annual day of sharing. When it came time to leave, Scholastica begged her brother not to go, but to remain through the night with her. He refused her request, gently reminding her of his requirement to sleep at the abbey. Seeing that he wouldn't relent, Scholastica laid her head on the table and began to cry and pray. As she poured out her heart to God, her tears were drowned out by the sound of a great storm that prevented both Benedict and his fellow monks from departing. Scholastica claimed that though her brother would not hear her request, God did. So Benedict and his men remained until morning, talking, praying, and sharing God's love with his joyful sister.

Read or tell the story of Saint Scholastica and Saint Benedict's final meeting. (*Optional:* Play sounds of a rainstorm during the reading or telling of the story.) Discuss God's unexpected answer to the sister's prayer to have a little more time with her brother. Explain to the students that this special gift from God meant a great deal to Scholastica because this turned out to be her last time on earth with her brother. Speculate that the reason this story is remembered and told is probably because the event meant a great deal to Benedict, as well, after his sister's death.

Explain that the group is going to have a part in recreating the story to help them remember God's gift to Saint Scholastica—a rainstorm that gave her a few more precious moments with the brother she loved. Play a game of "Rainstorm." Instruct the participants to stand in a circle. Tell them that there is to be no talking during this game. Appoint one person to lead the activity. The leader will begin each sound and "pass" it to the person on his or her right. The sound travels around the circle until everyone in the circle is helping to make it. The leader then begins a second sound which is passed around the circle. Say that each person should not begin the new sound until the person on the right gives the cue. It is important not to follow the leader's motions, or the group will not experience the progression of sounds that make this game effective. The sounds should take place in this order: silence, rubbing palms together in a circular motion, snapping fingers, slapping thighs, slapping thighs and stomping feet, slapping thighs, snapping fingers, rubbing palms together, silence.

Once the "Rainstorm" is over, remind the students that it is important to remember that we must love people more than rules, and it is good to understand that God sometimes answers our prayers in unexpected ways.

Naturalist Intelligence

Learn

By tracing their hands in the shape of a dove, participants will associate the story of Saint Scholastica's death with the symbol of her ascension into heaven.

Locate

Hole punches; Markers; Paper (heavy white); Paper doilies (white); Pencils; Ribbon or string; Scissors.

 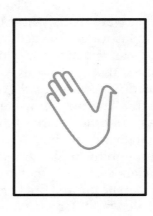

Lead

Saint Gregory the Great in his *Dialogues* tells the story of Scholastica's ascension into heaven. In 543 A.D. three days after their final visit when Scholastica had begged Benedict to stay just a little longer, Saint Scholastica died. When he found out about her death, Benedict was standing alone in his cell at the abbey at Monte Cassino. During his time of contemplation, Benedict lifted his eyes to the sky and beheld his sister's soul ascending into heaven in the form of a dove. He rejoiced to see her happy passage to eternity and gave thanks to God. Then he told the brothers of his vision and dispatched some of them to her convent to bring Scholastica's body to his monastery. Benedict lovingly placed his sister's body in the tomb he had prepared for his burial. His desire was that upon his death their earthly remains would be united, as their hearts had been on earth and their souls would be in heaven.

White doves are a common symbol for the Holy Spirit. Explain to the participants that a simple white dove can be formed from the shape of a hand. It can be used to tell the story of Scholastica's ascension into heaven and Benedict's vision of his sister's entrance into eternity.

Distribute heavy white paper, pencils, and scissors to the participants. Instruct each person to use a pencil to trace one hand onto the paper extending the thumb so it becomes the dove's head and closing the fingers to form the wing feathers. Tell the learners to cut out the shapes and to add details, such as eyes, with markers. Bits of paper lace, from white doilies, can be glued on for trim.

To form hangers for the doves, have each person punch a hole in the top of the shape. String a length of ribbon or yarn through the opening and tie the ends to form a loop. Suspend the doves and re-tell the story of Scholastica and Benedict.

Verbal/Linguistic Intelligence

Learn

By experiencing a first-person narrative, participants will comprehend biographical information regarding Saint Scholastica and connect the events of her life to a related Bible story, Matthew 8:23-27, and to the power of prayer.

Locate

Bible; Costume for "Benedictine Monk" storyteller; Story script.

Lead

Share the story of Saint Scholastica and tell the related Bible story as a first-person narrative. To enhance learning and to make the story memorable, dress a costumed character as a Benedictine monk to relate memories about Saint Scholastica.

Lead

"Benedictine Monk" Story Script
(adapted from Matthew 8:23-27)

Peace be with you! I bring you greetings from Monte Cassino. I am Brother Dexter. My Abbot, Benedict, named me Dexter because I am his "right-hand man." Dexter is Latin for "right hand," you see. It has been my privilege to serve our founder in many ways. Benedict is an amazing servant of God—and so is, or rather was, his sister, Scholastica.

I know, first hand, for I accompanied Benedict numerous times when he traveled the few miles once a year to meet with his beloved sister. The days with her always passed so quickly as I listened to them share their spiritual insights.

But last time, the visit ended very differently. Scholastica begged Benedict not to leave. He reminded her, gently, that our rules required us to spend the night within our abbey. Scholastica began to weep and to pray. As we prepared to leave, an incredible storm sprang up. Its brilliant flashes of lightning, great peals of thunder, and heavy downpour of rain made our trip impossible. It seemed that God himself intervened on Scholastica's behalf. She had gone over the Abbot's head—to God himself!

I was reminded of the Gospel story in which Jesus demonstrated God's power over wind and storm. One night on the Sea of Galilee, his disciples woke him because they were frightened by the weather. Jesus spoke but three words to rebuke the storm: "Peace, be still," he said. And the storm ceased. It seems to me that the God who calms storms can also send them if he chooses. Scholastica had confidence that God is Ruler over all—even the Rules of our Order. Now I see that God may have granted her this last joyful time with her brother because he knew that she was soon to return to his eternal embrace.

Benedict sent me to his sister again. Only this time it was my sad duty to bring her body back to the monastery for burial. Scholastica's earthly life was over. She died three days after their visit. Benedict placed her body in his own tomb where one day he, too, will be laid to rest. What a fitting end to these two lives whose earthly journeys have been so entwined. May their pattern of love and devotion remind us all that we, too, are brothers and sisters here on earth. And may we learn to celebrate—as they did— God's goodness every time we meet!

Visual/Spatial Intelligence

Learn

By illustrating their own version of her story, participants will visualize the important moments of Saint Scholastica's life.

Locate

Copy of book, *The Holy Twins—Benedict And Scholastica*, by Kathleen Norris and Tomie dePaola (New York: G. P. Putnam's Sons, 2001); Colored pencils or fine-tipped markers; Paper.

Lead

In their book, *The Holy Twins*, author Kathleen Norris and illustrator Tomie dePaola have created a beautiful version of the story of Scholastica and her brother, Benedict. Colorful and detailed drawings represent the lives of these siblings from their childhood to their death. Reading and seeing the scenes depicted in this children's book will help visual learners understand and appreciate the lives of these saints. Even more, participants who attempt to illustrate their own version of "The Holy Twins" will find an even deeper connection to the story.

Read the book to the listeners or review the story while highlighting the pictures that help to share the narrative. Ask the participants to watch for the moments that they think are important in Saint Scholastica's life. After sharing the published book, invite everyone to create a storyboard of the account.

First, distribute paper for the storyboard scenes. Have each student fold one piece of paper into thirds—like a business letter—and then fold the tri-fold in half. Tell the group to open the page that now has six "frames." Explain that they will draw six separate scenes from Saint Scholastica's life that they feel are the most memorable or the most important moments. Emphasize that artistry is not as important as communicating the idea. The students can use stick figures if they choose. Encourage them to add as much detail as possible, however.

Provide colored pencils or fine-tipped markers and give the learners time to develop their storyboards. Once the projects are completed, invite the artists to share their creations. Organize the class into small groups for discussion purposes or provide tacks or tape and have the artists post their pictures and walk around to view the different interpretations of Scholastica's life. Discuss which scenes seem to be most often repeated and why those seem so important to telling the saint's story.

An additional visual resource can be found at the website of the vocation's office of Saint Louis Abbey (www.stlouisabbey.org) entitled "The Illustrated Adventures of Saint Benedict." Episode 10 of this cartoon booklet features the story of Scholastica's storm. This format can serve as an example of how retelling a story by drawing our own version helps us visualize and remember important details.

MARCH
SAINT PATRICK

Biography

Patrick, born about 389 A.D. was the son of a Roman military officer who was stationed in Britain. When Patrick was sixteen, he was captured by raiders who took him across the sea to be sold into slavery in Ireland. As a young man, Patrick was not interested in religion, but while he worked as a shepherd for the Irish, he had many hardships which caused him to turn to God for help. During these six years of slavery, Patrick learned to pray and to trust God. When he finally escaped home to Britain, Patrick returned a changed man, ready to enter the priesthood.

Nearly fifteen years later, in a dream, Patrick heard the voices of the Irish people calling him to return to "walk with us again." Since Patrick already knew their language, the church agreed that he would be a good missionary to Ireland. Earlier missionaries had been killed in their attempts to bring the gospel to the Irish people, and Patrick's life was often in danger as well when he returned. The druid priests, who were magicians and wizards, sought to preserve their power over the people. They plotted against Patrick and attempted to kill him many times, but Patrick was always protected and spared.

Understanding Irish customs, Patrick knew that he must first convert the most powerful tribal chieftain. Once this was accomplished, Christianity began to take root in Ireland. Patrick remembered what it was like to be a slave, and so he treated all classes of people with Christ's love and respect. His courage and compassion made him a beloved leader, and through his efforts, many monasteries, convents, and churches were built. He died at Down in 460 A.D. In less than thirty years as a missionary, Patrick had brought about the conversion of Ireland.

Saint Patrick's feast day is March 17.

Mission

Patrick used the hardships life presented him as a way to discover what was truly important. He gave his life to God's service, and devoted himself to prayer. Even though at first he resisted going back to the land where he had been a prisoner, Patrick followed God's bidding and returned to the very people that had enslaved him in order to bring them God's love. Patrick lived and preached the Gospel of Jesus Christ and, without bloodshed, brought a new religion and a new way of life to an entire nation.

Legacy

Though born a Roman and a native of England, Patrick came to embody the heart and soul of Christian Ireland. His poetic prayers portray the delicate beauty of faith and yet are filled with the power of the Holy Spirit. Patrick's understanding and teaching of the Trinity, represented by the legend of the shamrock, still captures the imagination of the faithful today.

Bodily/Kinesthetic Intelligence

Learn

By retelling a Bible story, Luke 11:9-13, participants will understand the importance that Jesus, as well as Patrick, placed on the power of persistent prayer.

Locate

"Ask, Seek, Knock" Action Story; Bible(s).

Lead

One of the strengths of Saint Patrick was his belief in the power of prayer. Patrick's followers reported his sincere commitment to a life of prayer and to the importance that Jesus placed upon a life based on persistent prayer. In Luke 11, Jesus taught his disciples to pray and not to give up. Saint Patrick must have taken this Bible lesson to heart, especially verses nine through thirteen, where Jesus speaks of God answering our prayers.

As an engaging method of teaching today's disciples about Saint Patrick's commitment to prayer, involve the learners in retelling Luke 11:9-13. Explain that in an action story, the leader says a line and demonstrates the motions, and the participants repeat the words and the gestures.

"Ask, Seek, Knock" Action Story
(adapted from Luke 11:9-13)

The disciples wanted to learn to pray.
(Hold up praying hands.)

But prayer is more than the words we say.
(Cup hands to mouth.)

Jesus said we must ask each day
(Hold up hand like asking a question.)

And keep on asking when we pray.
(Support arm with other hand while continuing to "ask.")

In order to know how to live each day,
(Shrug shoulders; extend arms at sides.)

Jesus said we must seek God's way
(Put one hand above eyes and look left and right.)

The door of God's love isn't locked away
(Cross hands over chest)

We can knock and receive today
(Mime knocking on a door)

The gift of God's Spirit. Hip! Hip! Hooray!
(Open arms upward, then cheer aloud!)

Interpersonal Intelligence

Learn

By working together, participants will relate events from Patrick's life in the format of a cooperative game and enjoy a snack to celebrate their achievements.

Locate

Cups; Gummi snakes; Napkins; Plates; Shamrock-shaped green finger gelatin; Water.

Advance Preparation

Prepare green finger gelatin and cut it into shamrock shapes.

Lead

Provide an interpersonal activity to promote community building. Invite the participants to play a game to review facts from Saint Patrick's life while learning to encourage and support one another. Gather the group in one large or several smaller circles and explain that they will be playing a game called, "I'm Going to Ireland." Explain that each participant will begin by saying, "I'm going to Ireland, and I'm going to take . . . ". Then each person will name an item to take to the Emerald Isle. However, each person must follow the alphabet, choosing an item to take along that begins with the next letter. For example, the first person might say, "I'm going to Ireland, and I'm going to take an **a**tlas." The next might offer: "I'm going to Ireland, and I'm going to take an atlas and a **b**ag." Each person in succession must name all of the previous items before adding his or her own to the list. Play the game in a cooperative spirit; encourage those who are "stuck" to invite the group to help think of words. Congratulate the players for good ideas, smiling faces, or worthwhile contributions.

To challenge the group further, play the game another time requiring participants to name items that they believe Saint Patrick would take to the Emerald Isle. For example, "Saint Patrick's going to Ireland, and he's going to take an **a**ttitude of peace." The next might offer: "Saint Patrick's going to Ireland, and he's going to take an attitude of peace, and a **B**ible verse."

Continue the celebration of learning by connecting this group activity to snack time. Remind the group that Saint Patrick would have had to take **f**ood, **g**oodies, **l**unch, or **s**nacks. Invite participants to share refreshments.

Serve a snack of shamrock-shaped green finger gelatin. Help the learners understand the meaning of the treat. Remind the group that the shamrock is one plant with three different leaves, just as we worship one God whom we understand in three ways, as Father, Son, and Holy Spirit. Provide water to drink.

If desired, also offer Gummi snakes and share the legend that Patrick drove the snakes out of Ireland at the site of Croagh Patrick.

Offer a prayer such as "Come, Lord Jesus, be our guest, and let this food to us be blest" before eating the snack.

Intrapersonal Intelligence

Learn

By compiling a handmade book, participants will reflect on the prayers of Saint Patrick.

Locate

Awl, ice pick or hand drill; Copier; Darning or crewel needles; Examples of Celtic designs from the *Book of Kells*; Examples of Saint Patrick's prayers; Glue sticks; Heavy construction paper or cover stock; Heavy thread, such as buttonhole twist, carpet warp, or perle cotton; Lettering markers or pens; Paper (8 1/2" by 11"); Pencils; Rulers; Scissors; Scrap wood or wooden cutting board; Spring clips or clip clothespins.

Advance Preparation

Locate reference materials for Celtic designs. Photocopy examples of Saint Patrick's prayers.

Lead

After escaping from slavery in Ireland, young Patrick was educated at a French monastery and then studied religion with Saint Germanus, a French bishop. Later in his life, Patrick was determined to take the gospel back to pagan Ireland. The Irish people were converted to Christianity as a result of the work and teaching of Patrick. He is credited with founding more than 300 churches and with baptizing more than 120,000 Irish followers. The great educator introduced the Roman alphabet and Latin literature to the Irish people. At the time of Saint Patrick's death, many Irish monasteries were successful centers of learning.

Important information about Patrick's life comes from his own writings. He recounted his spiritual development in *Confession* and composed a hymn which is known as *Saint Patrick's Breastplate*. Make a booklet with a collection of the Saint's prayers. Demonstrate the process for the learners.

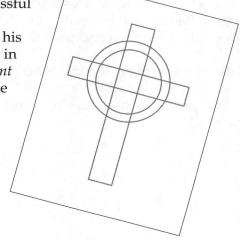

Fold several sheets of copy paper in half and stack them inside each other to make a book. Fold a piece of heavy construction paper or cover stock in half and place it on the outside of the folded stack. Use spring clips or clothespins to hold the pages in place. Open the book to the center, then mark five dots—evenly spaced—along the "ditch" or crease. Place a wooden cutting board under the book to prevent damage to the work surface. Use the awl, drill or needle to punch through the pencil marks. Be sure to make clean holes through all of the paper layers.

Cut heavy thread about three times longer than the book. Thread a large-eyed needle and sew the pages together with a running stitch. Start at the top of the book and sew in and out of the pre-punched holes allowing eight to ten inches of thread to extend beyond the top edge. At the fifth hole, sew the thread in the opposite direction filling in the spaces left by the running stitch. Pull the thread out at the center hole and remove the needle. Now thread the "tail" that is extending above the top edge and work that end back to the center hole. Remove the needle and tie the two loose ends together.

Decorate the front cover of the booklet with shamrocks or Celtic designs similar to the illustrations featured in the Book of Kells. Use markers or lettering pens to print the book's title. Write several of Saint Patrick's prayers on the book pages or cut photocopies to fit each page of the book.

Saint Patrick Prayers

Christ in Others

Christ in the lowly and meek,
Christ in the all-powerful,
Be in the heart of each to whom I speak,
In the mouth of each who speaks to me,
In all who draw near me,
Or see me, or hear me!

The Power of God

May the strength of God pilot us,
May the power of God preserve us,
May the wisdom of God instruct us,
May the hand of God protect us,
May the way of God direct us,
May the shield of God defend us,
May the host of God guard us
against snares of evil
and the temptations of the world.

The Protecting God

Lord be with us this day,
Within us to purify us;
Above us to draw us up;
Beneath us to sustain us;
Before us to lead us;
Behind us to restrain us;
Around us to protect us.

The Protection of Christ

Christ as a light
Illumine and guide me!

Christ as a shield overshadow and cover me!
Christ be under me! Christ be over me!
Christ be beside me,
On left hand and right!
Christ be before me, behind me, about me!
Christ, this day, be within and without me!

Provide supplies for the project and guide the group as they create handmade books.

Share the collections of prayers with other people and encourage the participants to try to memorize some of the selections.

Logical/Mathematical Intelligence

Learn

By following directions to select and organize images in a triptych, participants will demonstrate their understanding of Saint Patrick's teachings on the Trinity.

Locate

Braids, cording and trims; Brushes; Cardboard and Styrofoam scraps; Containers for paint; Copier; Gesso or acrylic-base paint; Glue; Gold paint; Hinges and tools or duct tape; Mat knife or craft saw; Paneling, plywood scraps or heavy cardboard or mat board; Paper; Pencils; Religious greeting cards or pictures; Rulers; Sandpaper; Scissors; Symbol patterns for the Trinity; Tempera or craft paints; Wood molding scraps.

Advance Preparation

Make copies of the symbols for the Trinity. Mark and cut wood or cardboard pieces ahead of time. Note that older children, teens and adults may enjoy cutting or sawing the triptych panels. Time and safety must be considered.

Lead

During his early days as a missionary, Patrick worked diligently to instruct the pagan people of Ireland about basic Christian beliefs. Patrick appeared before the pagan king and tried to explain the Trinity. In disbelief, the king asked, "How could three persons be in One?" Legends say Patrick used the shamrock to explain that the Father, Son, and Holy Spirit are three in one just as the shamrock is three leaves in one stem. Another example of "three-in-one" is artwork in the form of a triptych—three panels hinged to form one composition. The threefold art piece is constructed so that the two outside panels fold over the center like doors. This painting or carving usually depicts religious subject matter.

Explain that each participant will make a small triptych with symbols for the Father, Son, and Holy Spirit. Then, demonstrate the process for the project. Start by selecting three panels, arch-shaped or rectangular. Attach hardware hinges or join the edges with strips of duct tape.

Trace and cut symbols from scraps of cardboard or Styrofoam. Glue the shapes to the three panels, then add borders using various trims and molding scraps. Sand any rough edges of wood. Brush on Gesso or flat, white paint to cover all surfaces including the tape. Allow this base coat to dry. Paint the raised symbols and add touches of gold paint for background or borders. For additional texture, glue on gold braid or cording. Beautiful triptychs can be fashioned from religious pictures or greeting cards. Look for pictures that represent the Trinity or persons of the Trinity. Glue pictures over the painted panels and embellish them with gold trims.

Provide the supplies for the project and guide the group as they create their triptychs. Once the artwork is completed, find a place to display it so that others may learn about Saint Patrick's teachings on the Trinity.

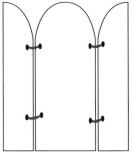

Musical/Rhythmic Intelligence

Learn

By learning and performing rhythmic movements to the "Peace Prayer," participants will further appreciate and interpret the meaning of "The Breastplate of Saint Patrick."

Locate

CD or Cassette of "Prayer for Peace" (David Haas); CD or Cassette player.

Lead

David Haas's rendition of "Peace Prayer" is based on words taken from the collection of writing known as the "Breastplate of Saint Patrick." Tradition teaches that Saint Patrick prayed continually for Christ's protection as he faced the dangers of his missionary work in Ireland. While the actual wording of the prayer may differ from translation to translation, the gist of Patrick's petition is for the Spirit of Christ to reside within, protect on all sides, and dwell around him each moment of each day. These words form the central message of Haas's arrangement.

Read selections or have participants share readings from Saint Patrick's original prayer. Discuss the meaning of the saint's request of God and the importance of this prayer for life today. Listen then to "Peace Prayer" and identify the words and phrases that could be interpreted with gesture and movement. Practice basic prayerful movements that would communicate each verse of the song. Only the first word in each line requires a new gesture. The basic prayer could be interpreted as follows:

Peace before us
(Extend arms, palms up, in front of body.)

Peace behind us
(Extend arms, palms up, behind body.)

Peace under our feet
(Bend knees and sweep arms along sides of feet.)

Peace within us
(Stand, bringing arms out, then touch hands to chest.)

Peace over us
(Raise arms over head, touching fingers together.)

Let all around us be peace
(Extend arms forward and turn in place.)

For each verse add the specific gesture for peace, light, and Christ. For example:

Peace
(Clasp hands together, alternating right hand on top, then left. Open hands and sweep palms down and to opposite sides.)

Light
(Cup left hand, place back of right hand in left palm, fingers together pointing up. Raise right hand slightly above left, quickly opening fingers at the same time.)

Christ
(Place parallel hands, palms facing, in front of chest; touch the left palm with middle finger of right hand, then touch right palm with middle finger of left hand.)

Practice until all can share the movements together as a prayer for peace.

Naturalist Intelligence

Learn

By using elements found in nature to develop a symbolic picture, participants will recreate Saint Patrick's methods for sharing the Christian message.

Locate

Dark blue construction paper and/or photosensitive paper; Natural materials such as grasses, flowers, shamrocks, or stones; Pattern for Celtic cross; Tape.

Lead

Saint Patrick brought Christianity to Ireland in a natural way, without war or bloodshed. He used beliefs and customs that the Celtic people already held and simply added the further meaning revealed in the life of Christ. All of nature gave Saint Patrick methods of teaching God's truth to people who lived in the darkness of fear and magic.

Once King Laoghaire and his Druid priests were celebrating a great pagan festival at the hill of Tara. No fire was to be lit until the king's fire; but on the night before Easter, Patrick lit the holy Paschal fire on the hill of Slane. The blaze could be seen throughout the countryside, and the king was furious. When Patrick heard of the king's anger, he answered in the psalmist's words proclaiming, "... we will walk in the name of our God." Walking safely to the king's court despite threats on his life, Patrick began to win over some of the king's own followers. They began to understand that the light of the fire represented Jesus, the Light of the World.

Saint Patrick also helped the Celts to transform their worship of natural symbols, like the circle of the sun. He helped them to see the sun as a symbol of light, representing God's Son who brought eternal life. Thus, the Celtic cross shows a circle behind a Latin cross, standing for eternal life in the light of Christ.

As a reminder of Saint Patrick's gentle teaching and use of nature to share God's truth, invite the participants to create symbols for display. In advance or as a group, collect natural materials like flowers, grasses, shamrocks, or stones. Cut out the shape of a Celtic cross for a pattern. Distribute dark blue construction paper or photo-sensitive paper and demonstrate how to design an arrangement that symbolizes a message from God. Use circles of tape on the back to hold the materials in place, but do not let any tape show. Direct the learners to place the construction paper in the sun all day, or follow the package directions if using photo-sensitive paper. After the timed exposure, carefully remove the pattern to reveal the design created by the effects of the sun. Place the projects in a location where others may see the symbols and have an opportunity to hear an explanation of their meaning.

Verbal/Linguistic Intelligence

Learn

By experiencing a first-person narrative, participants will comprehend biographical information regarding Saint Patrick and connect the events of his life to a related Bible story, Luke 11:9-13, and to the importance of prayer.

Locate

Bible; Costume for "Minstrel" Storyteller; Shamrock (artificial symbol or live plant); Shamrock stickers (one per participant); Story Script.

Lead

Share the story of Saint Patrick and tell the related Bible story as a first-person narrative. To enhance learning and to make the story memorable, a costumed "Minstrel" should relate memories about his favorite saint, Patrick.

"Minstrel" Story Script
(adapted from: Luke 11:9-13)

The "minstrel" storyteller enters singing new words to the tune of "Michael Row The Boat Ashore."

"Three in One, Yet One in Three
Alleluia."
"'Tis the blessed Trinity
Alleluia."

Greetings pilgrims! My name is Quinn, that is a Celtic word which means "wise." I hear that you have been learning about Ireland's patron saint, Saint Patrick. He also was very wise. In fact, the song I was just singing reflects the wise words of Saint Patrick. I am a minstrel you know. That means I travel around putting words to music to entertain people. Let me teach you the "Three-in-One" song. (Practice and sing the song together several times.)

Wonderful! Maybe some of you should become minstrels, too! Saint Patrick wasn't exactly a minstrel, but he traveled through Ireland sharing his words of wisdom and his prayers with the people. One bit of wisdom Patrick shared was a simple way to understand the Christian belief of the Trinity: God as Father, Son, and Holy Spirit. (Use a shamrock to tell the story.)

You see, the shamrock grows plentifully in Ireland. And when the people thought Patrick was talking about three different gods, he showed them the leaf of the shamrock plant. "How many plants is this?" he asked them. Of course, they answered, "Only one." "Yet it has three leaves in one stem," Saint Patrick explained. "We worship only one God, yet we understand our God in three ways: God our Creator, God our Savior, and God our Helper." In this way, the shamrock came to represent the Trinity, God the Father, Son, and Holy Spirit. (Sing the song again.)

The story of the shamrock is just one of the famous stories from the life of Saint Patrick. He had many adventures and dangers in his experiences as a missionary. Saint Patrick could have never accomplished all that he did in Ireland without the power of prayer and the presence of the Holy Spirit helping him.

Jesus taught his disciples about the importance of prayer. He told them that they had to ask God, like a child would ask a loving parent, for what they needed. Jesus promised his disciples—and that includes Saint Patrick and you and me—that God would give the gift of the Holy Spirit to those who ask. Saint Patrick wrote that he sometimes said a hundred prayers a day. That is really persistence in prayer. No wonder the power of God's Holy Spirit was with him!

Maybe you will learn to say some of the prayers of Saint Patrick. Even more importantly, you can learn to pray yourselves to our loving God who will send the Holy Spirit to be with you wherever you travel in life.

(Have the minstrel give each child a shamrock sticker or symbol to keep. The minstrel storyteller exits singing.)

Visual/Spatial Intelligence

Learn

Through the creation of a metal-tooled, Celtic cross, the participants will associate the shape with the meaning of the traditional Irish symbol. They will also make further connections by relating the Celtic cross to Patrick's religious teachings.

Locate

Batting or clay; Clear lacquer (Check with craft supply dealer or paint store for non-toxic products); Copier; Copper escutcheon pins or standard staples; Copper tooling foil or other heavy duty foil; Exacto knives; Fine steel wool; Liver of sulfur (available at art stores or pharmacies); Magazines or newspapers; Old paint brushes or cotton swabs; Paper; Pattern for Celtic cross; Pencil stubs, "dead" ballpoint pens, and plastic or wooden spoons; Pencils; Picture hangers; Rags; Scissors; Tack hammer or stapler; Tape; Wood pieces or heavy mat boards; Wooden tools for metal tooling or dowel rods, wooden styluses, or cuticle sticks.

Advance Preparation

Cut copper foil to proper size. Cut wood or mat board bases slightly larger than the copper rectangles. Make copies of Celtic cross pattern (enlarge to about 4" x 6").

Lead

An ancient people known as Celts lived in Ireland. They originated a cross that has become a traditional Irish symbol. The Celtic cross is upright with a circle behind the crossbeam. Examples of the Celtic cross are seen all over Ireland in landmarks as well as other artwork. The circle represents eternal life, thus many cemeteries in Ireland and Britain have marked graves with Celtic crosses. The custom was brought to America with the early settlers and is still used in cemeteries today.

Many of the crosses were made of stone with elaborately carved or engraved designs. Some of the crosses were fashioned and embellished by metalworkers. Celtic crosses are still a favorite emblem for jewelry and other decorative pieces.

Explain that each participant will design a Celtic cross plaque using the ancient process of repousse also known as tooling, modeling or embossing. Demonstrate the process for the project. Trace the cross pattern onto a piece of paper or use a photocopy of the design. Select a piece of copper foil for the project. Tape the corners of the paper cross pattern to the copper piece so the image will not shift. Place the pattern and copper on a magazine or a pad of newspaper.

Trace all of the lines by pressing hard with an embossing stylus or pencil which has a dull point. Turn the metal over to see if all of the lines have been traced. Remove the paper design and go over the same outline directly on the metal.

Place the traced design face down on the pad and begin the embossing or repousse process. Use the "spoon" end of the special modeling tool or the bowl of a small spoon to press over all of the parts that will be raised in relief. Turn the piece right side up, move to a hard surface and continue the process by rubbing around the cross to smooth the background away from the relief shape. Pushing into the pad allows for the metal sheet to stretch; pressing over the copper on a hard surface flattens bumps and ripples. Continue working on both sides of the metal until the design is clearly defined. Use care not to push in the raised image while smoothing the background area. Also, be careful to avoid sharp edges of the metal piece.

For a bright finish, polish the cooper with steel wool and apply lacquer to maintain the shine. Copper foil can be given an antique finish by brushing on liver of sulfur with an old brush or cotton swab. When the solution is thoroughly dry, buff relief the design with steel wool, wipe with a clean rag, and apply lacquer to the surface to prevent further oxidation.

To prevent the raised Celtic cross design from denting, fill in the pressed areas on the back side with clay or batting before mounting. Center the repousse piece on the wooden or mat board base and tack it in place with a hammer and tiny escutcheon pins or staples. Wooden bases could be sanded and stained before the mounting step. Attach a picture hanger to the back of the base.

Provide supplies for the project and guide the group as they create their crosses.

For a less involved process, consider metal tooling kits which are available through craft supply catalogs. Heavy duty aluminum foil in rolls or available in baking pans may be used in place of copper. Eliminate the oxidizing, polishing, and lacquering steps.

APRIL
SAINT CATHERINE OF SIENA

Biography

In 1347, Catherine was born in Siena, Italy, one of twin daughters, the twenty-third and twenty-fourth children of Giacomo and Lapa Benincasa. Her father was a successful businessman, operating his own dye shop on the first floor of the family home. Tradition teaches that Catherine was only six years old when she had her first vision. As she and her brother were walking home from their older sister's house, Catherine looked toward the Church of San Domenico and saw a vision of Jesus and the apostles. She told no one of her experience at the time, but her impression of God's call on her life never left. When a year later she saw Mary with her Son, Catherine pledged herself to Jesus and understood that she would never marry.

At age 12, still having told no one of her intent to serve God, her parents began to encourage her to look for a husband. Catherine tried to resist, but finally had to explain her commitment to Christ, even cutting off all her hair to prove her determination not to marry. Her mother fired the family servant and forced Catherine to perform all the household duties so that she would have no time to pray. Catherine learned to make a space in her heart where she could be alone with God in prayer while she did the cooking and the cleaning. Finally, her father saw a white dove appear above Catherine's head and decided that he would support her in her vow to God. He hired a servant to do the work and allowed Catherine to have her room back so that she could pray in private.

For three years, Catherine meditated in her room—she could neither read nor write—leaving only to go to confession and to Mass. At eighteen, Catherine asked for the black-and-white Dominican habit, pronounced her vows as a lay member of the order, and practiced a cloistered life in her own home. Catherine prayed for God to help her learn to read, and she soon began to read fluently and was able to recite the Divine Office. In 1367, Jesus appeared to Catherine and called her to serve the poor and the sick people of Siena. Although she lacked formal education, Catherine dedicated the rest of her life to providing for the needs of God's people and maintaining the unity of the church.

In 1380, at the age of 33, Catherine suffered a stroke and died. Her feast day is observed on April 29.

Mission

Catherine's life was shaped by her visions. Her complete dedication to Christ led her to reach out to sick and sinful people, to serve as arbitrator in disputes, and to seek reform in the church. Her life reflects her belief that mystical union with God knits us to the world and its people. At the young age of 24, Catherine was able to inspire others, even learned men, to look to her for spiritual direction. Her message of repentance and reconciliation drew many to follow her and support her efforts to care for the poor and needy.

Legacy

Catherine's efforts to restore unity to the church and to record her visions of God's love and mercy form her legacy. In 1376, when the church was divided over the pope's residing in France, Catherine volunteered to speak to Pope Gregory XI. She was able to remind him of his promise to God to return to Rome and strengthened his resolve to do so. Catherine also founded a monastery of cloistered Dominican sisters at the fortress at Belcaro. But perhaps her greatest contribution was through her dictation of her mystical experiences recorded in her book *The Dialogue*. After Pope Gregory's death, Catherine was also called to Rome by Pope Urban VI to try to increase support for his papacy and to bring healing to the church. Catherine moved to Rome with a group of her followers and remained there until her death. Pope Pius II canonized Catherine in 1461; in 1970, she became one of two women to be named a Doctor of the Church.

Bodily/Kinesthetic Intelligence

Learn

By modeling clay into a visible prayer, participants will experience the truth of Saint Catherine's life that prayer is a force that shapes and changes us.

Locate

Cassette or CD player; Cassette tape or CD of tranquil music without sung lyrics; Modeling clay.

Lead

Prayer shaped Catherine's life. From her earliest awareness of God's call, Catherine wanted nothing more than to be alone with God and to pray without ceasing. Through her devotion to prayer and her growing intimacy with God, Catherine came to understand that to love God was to reach out to others. Her prayer changed her from a recluse to a servant. Once Catherine began to work among God's people, their needs and concerns began to shape her prayers. By working in the church, by tending to the poor, by suffering with those who were persecuted, Catherine found the focus for her prayer life. Thus, Catherine's prayer shaped her activities, and her activities shaped her prayer.

This interrelationship of prayer and participation should exist in our lives today. To help the students understand the connection between a life of quiet prayer and a life of active involvement, present them with an opportunity to use modeling clay to sculpt a prayer.

Explain that they are going to experience praying with clay. Begin playing tranquil music and tell the participants that they are to allow the music and the clay to help shape their prayers. Tell them that they should remain quiet as they share in this experience. Distribute a lump of clay to each person. Ask them to roll the clay into a ball and to knead it until it can be easily shaped. While the students do this, they should picture someone for whom they wish to pray, a situation about which they plan to pray, or an answer to prayer for which they would like to give thanks. Once the clay is ready, remind the group to begin shaping their prayer and forming the clay to represent the person or situation that is the focus of their meditation. Allow time and quiet for this process. When it seems appropriate, fade the music, and ask the participants to place their "shaped prayers" on display.

Invite the participants to tell the stories of their prayers. Ask them to share what they experienced as they worked with the clay and to express the thoughts they had as they shaped their prayers. Discuss the changes that happened as they tried to make their prayers visible. Explain that as Saint Catherine shaped her prayer, her prayer began to shape her life.

Interpersonal Intelligence

Learn

By creating thank-you notes for the mentors in their lives, participants will realize the impact that Saint Catherine of Siena's letters had on many people.

Locate

Card stock or index cards, 4" x 6"; Colored pencils or fine-tipped markers, including black; Dictionary; Pencils; Pens; Rulers; Scissors.

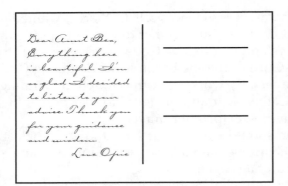 

Lead

Saint Catherine of Siena was one of the most brilliant theological minds of her day, although she never had any formal education. She acquired a reputation as a person of immense insight and sound judgment. People from all walks of life sought her spiritual advice, both in person and by letter. Throughout her lifetime, Catherine wrote approximately 400 letters to popes and sovereigns, rulers of republics and leaders of armies, as well as men and women in the cloister and peasants and merchants in the community.

Through her letter writing, Catherine of Siena served as a mentor to many people. Invite a volunteer to look up the word "mentor" in a dictionary. It may be defined as a person who is a coach, counselor, friend, guide, instructor, model, teacher, trainer or tutor for someone else. Catherine fit all of these descriptions. Most people have a mentor, probably many of them, in fact. Invite the pupils to think of people who have made an impact on their lives. It might be a catechist or weekday schoolteacher, camp counselor, parent, grandparent, or friend. Ask each person to reflect on the special qualities of one person and to consider ways that the individual has affected his or her life. Design a "mini-letter" in the form of a handmade postcard and use it to say thank you to this mentor. Demonstrate the process for the students.

To create a postcard, cut a four-inch by six-inch piece from card stock or use a blank index card. On one side of the card stock, create the back of a postcard. Using a ruler, draw a straight line down the center of the card to divide one half for the address and the other half for the greeting. On the half for the address—the right side—use a ruler to draw three straight horizontal lines on the lower half of the card. In the "message" section, write a note of appreciation to the mentor. On the front side of the card, print the words "Thank You" and draw a picture. Color the illustration with markers or pencils. Write the address on the card, add a postage stamp, and mail the postcard.

Provide supplies for the project and guide the group as they create personal messages to their mentors. Invite the learners to offer an individual or a group prayer to thank God for the mentors in their lives.

Intrapersonal Intelligence

Learn

By creating a heart pocket, participants will practice the teachings of Saint Catherine of Siena as they seek to find inner peace in the midst of life.

Locate

Foam meat or produce trays (well washed), various colors; 6″ heart patterns; Hole punches; Markers; Paper, cut into small slips; Pencils; Pens; Ribbon or yarn; Scissors.

Lead

When Catherine finally informed her family that she did not intend to marry, but rather remain single and serve God, her parents were angry. They tried to persuade her to accept suitors, so Catherine cut off her hair to make herself undesirable. Her mother's response was to take away Catherine's private bedroom so that she would have no place for meditation and prayer. Catherine's mother also fired the family servant and gave all of the household duties to Catherine so that she would have no time to pursue her spiritual devotion. Instead of defeating Catherine's spirit, her mother's tactics caused Catherine to turn more deeply to God for help. God's answer to Catherine was that she possessed an inner "cell" or "closet," a place in her heart where she and God could continually be together. Learning to retreat within her self gave Catherine a way to find God's abiding peace despite the external pressures of life. Later in life, Catherine shared her belief that everyone could find God's peace within their own hearts.

Catherine's belief was that God wants to meet with us in the center of our lives. Explain to the participants that each person has the power to invite God into his or her heart. There is a space deep within that we must open to God by seeking the indwelling presence of the Holy Spirit. To help make this spiritual concept more real to the learners, tell them that they will create a heart-shaped pocket to represent their inner space. The pocket, and its contents, will serve to remind them that they can be alone with God any time they wish.

Invite each person to select a foam tray. Provide heart patterns, pencils, and scissors. Tell the learners to use a pencil to trace the heart pattern on the foam and to cut out the shape. Then have them cut the bottom half of another six-inch heart from foam—the same color or a different color. Provide hole punches and guide the group as they punch holes evenly around the edge of the heart. Direct them to lay the large heart over the half-heart, mark holes, and punch openings in the smaller shape. Demonstrate how to use a piece of ribbon or yarn to stitch the two pieces together, lacing through each hole. Guide the group as they complete this step.

Provide slips of paper and markers or pens and invite the participants to write words and to draw pictures to serve as reminders of how to find God in the "busy-ness" of life. Examples include copying Scripture verses related to prayer, like "Pray in secret" (Matthew 6:6) or "Pray always" (Luke 18:1). The slips could contain words like "Come into my heart, Jesus" to offer as a breath prayer. Explain that they should say the phrase as they inhale and feel God's presence as they exhale. Other suggestions might be to draw pictures of people or situations that they want God to bless. Explain that picturing their thoughts and concerns given to God is a form of meditation.

Close by reminding the participants that our private time with God strengthens us for life in the world. Tell the listeners to find their inner "cell" or "closet," the quite place where God dwells within them. Instruct the group to remain quiet for one minute and to allow God's peace to fill their hearts. Provide sixty seconds of silent reflection. Encourage the students to take their heart pockets home as a reminder to continue to seek God within themselves.

Logical/Mathematical Intelligence

Learn

By working together to construct a weaving, participants will appreciate the combination of Saint Catherine of Siena's commitment to truth and her love for God and the church.

Locate

Basket or box; Cardboard, 3' x 5'; Exacto or utility knife; Heavy string; Markers; Materials such as cloth strips, heavy yarns, paper strips, plastic bags and wide ribbon; Round head brass fasteners (brads), three-quarter inch; Scissors; Slats, 1' wooden.

Advance Preparation

Prepare the cardboard by poking holes into the top and bottom of the piece with your knife. These should be placed approximately three inches apart. Into each hole push a three-quarter inch brad. Tying off the string around the first brad, zigzag the heavy string around the brads. Tie off the string around the last brad. Cut the materials into strips one inch wide and four to five feet long. Place the pieces in a basket or box.

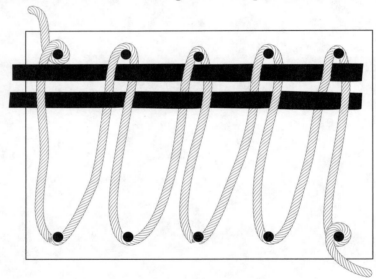

Lead

Catherine took the Dominican motto "*Veritas*" or "Truth" as her own. She considered the commitment to truth to be the root of the spiritual life, beginning with self-knowledge. Catherine believed that we must meet God in the depth of our "inner cell" and humble ourselves before God's greatness. For Catherine, from this solitude with God came the strength to use her free will to act on God's behalf. Catherine believed that if something needed saying or doing, she had to risk a response. While she spoke against the schism in the Church, she also prayed daily—often all day—for the Church's unity. Catherine's life was a weaving of action and reflection, of speaking out and of praying in silence. Her efforts to weave a new tomorrow for the church required her to be both emotionally and spiritually strong. Even though she was a woman at a time when women leaders were rare and was physically ill and weak, Catherine challenged the leaders of the Church who needed God's correction and helped bring about spiritual reform in her time.

Like Catherine, we must seek to know God through prayer, study of scripture, and obedience to the Holy Spirit. God calls people in every generation to seek God's Truth and to speak for the unity of God's people. Discuss ways that Christians can work today to bring the truth of God's love to all people. Consider ideas like forming a youth Bible study or a children's prayer group. Talk about community needs such as a tutoring program or a nursing home pen pal project. Review ways to invite people to church such as sidewalk art or seasonal banners outside of the building. Then create a weaving to help the participants visualize how their individual contributions can be combined to work to bring the truth of God's love to all people.

Explain that weaving is an art form that combines a variety of strands or pieces into a beautiful blend of texture, fabric, and design. Show the participants the background piece and explain that, individually and collectively, they will be weaving a new tomorrow for their church.

Ask each person to pick a piece of material from the basket or box. Distribute permanent markers and ask them to write on the strip one way in which they will work to share the truth of God's love with others. The ideas could include being honest in class, meeting a need in the community, or writing a letter to a homebound parishioner. Offer each person an opportunity to read his or her idea and to weave the piece into the base. Periodically place a wooden slat into the weaving to make it more secure.

As the weaving is taking place, discuss how this project symbolizes each person's part in weaving a new tomorrow, and how it becomes possible when many people work together. Display the completed piece in a prominent location.

Musical/Rhythmic Intelligence

Learn

By learning the words to a contemporary hymn, participants will understand Saint Catherine of Siena's philosophy that we must love God by serving others in Jesus' name.

Locate

Music for "Jesu, Jesu, Fill Us With Your Love" (Adapted by Tom Colvin, arranged by Jane Marshall)

Lead

At first, Catherine of Siena thought that she could show her devotion to God by leading a secluded life of prayer and meditation. Catherine lived for three years in the isolation of her room, leaving just to go to confession or to Mass. Then. suddenly, Jesus gave her a new understanding of what she should do to be a faithful Christian. To be one with Christ required Jesus' followers to be one with God's world. Catherine left her solitude to venture out to serve the poor and the needy. She began tending terminally ill patients at the hospital. When Catherine heard the screams of prisoners being taken to their execution, she began ministering to those imprisoned, helping them to prepare for death. During the outbreak of the plague, Catherine attended to the family members of the sick. Her concern was always for those who were outcasts, those who needed to know God's love and experience God's forgiveness. For Catherine, to love God meant serving others in Jesus' name.

A contemporary hymn, "Jesu, Jesu, Fill Us With Your Love," captures this important lesson. Sing the song or play it for the participants and invite them to learn the words and the music. Then share the story behind the hymn. A man named Thomas Colvin was a missionary in Africa during the 1960s. At that time a group of new Christians brought him a tune that was traditionally used as a love song in Ghana. They thought it might make a good Christian song to sing. So Tom Colvin rewrote the words to express the type of love Jesus came to teach us. From that simple folk tune came the popular contemporary hymn, "Jesu, Jesu, Fill Us With Your Love."

In many ways, that is just what Jesus did with the idea people had about loving God. Before Jesus taught them better, his disciples thought that loving God was something they did by themselves—praying, offering sacrifices, paying tithes, and keeping the Ten Commandments. Jesus said that—while those were good practices—to truly love God required us to serve one another. If we follow Jesus, we will show we love God by sharing who we are and what we have with everyone around us, whether it's the person next door or someone far away.

That is the message of Tom Colvin's words sung to the old Ghanian folk song. And that is the message of Jesus, who showed what it meant to love God by giving his life for us.

Naturalist Intelligence

Learn

By participating in a guided meditation, learners can understand Saint Catherine of Siena's vision of Jesus as the bridge between heaven and earth.

Locate

Markers; Materials for building "bridges" such as blocks, Lego, Tinker Toys or toothpicks; Paper; Photos of bridges.

Lead

Saint Catherine of Siena spent much time in meditation, focusing on God's gift of Jesus and Jesus' gift to humanity. She used many images in her writings to help others understand God's great love. One image God gave Catherine was of Jesus as the bridge between God and humankind. Catherine probably envisioned a structure like the Ponte Vecchio Bridge over the Arno River in Florence, Italy. The symbolism of the bridge formed the key image in *The Dialogue*, Catherine's greatest written work. As a bridge over sin and death, Jesus helps us cross over the stormy seas of life to find God's love and forgiveness, and—eventually—to find our way from earth to heaven.

To help the students create a vision of Jesus as the bridge to God, introduce a guided imagery activity. Explain that the function of a bridge is to connect two areas and to enable people and things to get from one place to another. Begin by having the students brainstorm different kinds of bridges, including examples like a drawbridge, suspension bridge, or toll bridge. Then offer illustrations, paintings and photographs of different forms of bridges. Explain that everyone is going to use his or her imagination to visit a place that needs a bridge. Use the script for the "Guided Meditation" to inspire their imaginary visit. Consider dimming the lights, playing reflective music, and creating a relaxed setting before beginning the activity.

Guided Meditation

Please close your eyes and let your mind and spirit get very quiet. Take a deep breath and ask God to be present as we spend these moments in our imaginations. I will guide your thoughts as we stay quiet and think about a beautiful place in God's world near a great river.

Imagine all the scenery that would be around you. What plants can you see? What color is the water? Create the picture in your mind and let yourself imagine you are there. Now, imagine that you can see across to the other side of the river. On the other bank you can view an even more beautiful place. You understand that this place is heaven, and you wish that you could get there. But you cannot get across the great river that separates you from the other shore. You see someone standing on the other side. It is Jesus. He waves to you and seems to know what you need. Jesus begins to build a bridge between heaven and your place on the other side of the river. What kind of bridge is Jesus building? See the bridge slowly take shape as Jesus works to span the distance between you and God. Finally, the bridge is complete. You can now cross over the river.

Jesus walks toward you across the bridge ready to help you find your way to heaven. You want to say thank you that Jesus has cared enough to build a bridge just for you. What would you say to Jesus? Tell him what is in your heart. Now, Jesus reminds you that this bridge between you and God is always there for you to use. You just have to picture this place in your mind and know that he will guide you over the rivers that separate you from God. Look around again so that you can remember what this place and this bridge look like. Then, when you are ready, you may open your eyes and come back to this time and place, ready to share the image God gave you.

After the "Guided Meditation," invite the students to build the bridge they imagined from materials such as blocks, Lego, Tinker Toys, or toothpicks. Or, encourage them to draw a picture or to write a story on a piece of paper. Let volunteers share their creations and explain what kind of bridge they saw in their imaginations. Discuss Saint Catherine of Siena's vision of the bridge to God that Jesus provides for us.

Verbal/Linguistic Intelligence

Learn

By experiencing a first-person narrative, participants will comprehend biographical information regarding Saint Catherine of Siena and connect the events of her life to a related Bible story about Mary Magdalene, John 20:1-18, and to their own commitment to God.

Locate

Bible; Costume for "Biographer" Storyteller; Story script.

Lead

Share the story of Saint Catherine of Siena and tell the related Bible story about Mary Magdalene as a first-person narrative. To enhance learning and to make the story memorable, a costumed character representing Raymond of Capua, Catherine's "biographer," should relate memories about his favorite Saint, Catherine.

"Biographer" Story Script
(adapted from: John 20:1-18)

Grace to you and peace! I am Raymond of Capua, a Dominican and chaplain to a great follower of our Lord named Catherine of Siena. Perhaps my parents were prophetic when they named me Raymond, for the meaning behind it is "great protector." It has been my privilege to work with Catherine as her confessor and spiritual director, and I would like to think as her earthly "great protector." She was a woman of courage and faith, and it has been my joy to be her biographer, to write the amazing story of what I saw and heard as she lived each moment for God.

Writing her biography, I find the greatest challenge to be how to select which stories to share—there are so many! I believe people must be made to understand the power that Catherine had in bringing others to the faith. I remember once in Pisa that so many people came to hear this unassuming woman preach that penitents lined up outside the church and past the city gates. I had to ask for other priests to come and help us hear all the confessions! It was after this great event that Catherine received a mighty sign from God. She was praying in front of the crucifix in Pisa in the Church of Santa Cristina when Jesus spoke to her from the cross. In that moment the wounds of Christ, the stigmata, appeared upon her hands and feet. Although she was aware of sharing in Christ's suffering, the wounds remained invisible to others until her death.

Catherine's compassion for others reminds me of another powerful woman who followed Christ. Her story is found in the Bible. She was a woman who knew what it meant to be forgiven, for Christ had cast seven demons out of her. She became one of his most devoted followers. In fact, it was this woman that the gospel of John teaches was the first to see Christ after his resurrection. Jesus revealed himself to her as she stood praying at the tomb, calling her name, "Mary!" Do you know the story of Mary Magdalene? If you do, you know why I say Catherine reminds me of this early disciple. Mary Magdalene surely would have had the same passion for telling others of God's love and forgiveness. Though a woman, Mary was entrusted with the Good News of Easter morning, and as the first to see Jesus alive, it became her job to go and tell the others what God had accomplished. Jesus made it clear that women were an important part of his mission. Catherine helped me learn that lesson, just as Mary must have helped Peter and the other disciples understand that all of God's people must be about spreading the joy of Christ's love and triumphant mercy. All of us are called to be the "great protectors" of that truth! Catherine taught me. I have told you her story. Now you must share it, too. Remember Christ's words to Mary: "Go and tell the others!"

Visual/Spatial Intelligence

Learn

By designing a mobile representing the two crowns that Catherine was offered, participants will consider the Saint's choice to serve Jesus as well as their own response to the Lord.

Locate

Duplicating equipment; Hole punches; Illustration of crown of thorns; Markers; Pattern for crown of gold; Poster board, gold or yellow; Ribbon, string, or yarn; Scissors; Staples; Staplers.

Advance Preparation

Enlarge the crown of gold pattern to the desired size and duplicate one copy for each participant. Reproduce four to six crowns of thorn for each student.

Lead

Catherine reported that Jesus appeared to her in a vision and presented two crowns: one made of gold and one made of thorns. He asked her to choose which crown she preferred for life and which one she preferred for eternity. Catherine chose to live on earth in the pattern of Jesus, accepting the pain and suffering that the crown of thorns represented. To Catherine, it seemed a delight to follow in Christ's pattern of service and sacrifice and to know that the joy of the golden crown awaited her in eternity. For Catherine, life on earth was a balance of prayer and service, and the suffering in the present was outweighed by the glory of the life to come.

Help the participants remember Catherine's choice to accept the suffering of the present life as a sacrifice for God by creating a crown mobile. Explain that Catherine understood that her eternal reward was a crown of gold, but that she chose to follow Christ's pattern of service to others for her life on earth. Recall that she did not serve others in order to receive the crown of gold, but in order to be like Jesus.

Provide a copy of the crown of gold pattern and a piece of poster board for each student. Offer pencils and scissors to share. Tell the group to trace the crown pattern onto the poster board and to cut out the shape. Supply paper punches and have the learners evenly space four to six holes across the bottom of the crown as well as one on each half of the top of the shape.

Share stories about the deeds that Catherine accomplished in her life. Brainstorm ways in which these stories show how Catherine accepted her crown of thorns on earth. Ideas could include facts such as: she visited the sick, she ministered to those in prison, she fed the poor, she worked to build bridges between people, she fasted, she wrote letters, she was a peacemaker, she prayed constantly for the church. Distribute four to six copies of the crown of thorns and several markers to each person. Ask everyone to write one of Catherine's deeds on each piece. Provide hole punches and have everyone punch a hole in the top of each crown of thorns.

Cut pieces of ribbon, string, or yarn in varying lengths. Offer each mobile-maker a piece for each crown of thorns. Tell them to attach one end of each string to a crown of thorns and to tie the other end through the pre-punched holes in the bottom of the crown of gold.

Help the participants staple the ends of their poster board to form the crown shape. Offer an additional piece of string and demonstrate how to use it to form a hanger for the mobile.

Invite the students to display their completed projects, to discuss the choice that Catherine made between the two crowns, and to consider which crown each person might select.

MAY
SAINT JOAN OF ARC

Biography

Joan of Arc, also known as Jeanne d'Arc, was born in Domremy near the province of Lorraine, France on January 6, 1412. Her parents, Jacques d'Arc and Isabelle Romee, were peasant farmers. Joan and her family were illiterate, but devout in their faith. As a young girl, she began hearing the voices of Saint Catherine of Alexandria, Saint Margaret of Antioch, and Saint Michael the Archangel. They told Joan marvelous predictions of her future—that she would help save France. They challenged her to raise the siege of Orleans, conduct the Dauphin Charles to Rheims for his coronation as king, and drive the English from the country. For a young girl whose life revolved around tending sheep and spinning wool, such things seemed impossible.

However, in May of 1428, the voices urged her to go to Charles, the heir to the French throne. Charles had been too fearful to try to claim his crown from the English King and the French Duke of Burgundy who was siding with the English against Charles. Joan convinced the French leaders to give her a small army and, with the successful siege of Orleans on May 8, 1429, she began to rally French troops and enjoy great military victories. Charles VII was crowned King of France on July 17, 1429, with Joan at his side. However, the king began to ignore Joan, and ultimately, in May of 1430, as she was leading a campaign, she was captured. The King of France did nothing to save her, and eventually Joan was turned over to the English. At the age of nineteen, on May 30, 1431, Joan was burned at the stake as a heretic in Rouen's market square. After a review of the verdict against Joan in 1456, she was exonerated of all guilt. Joan was finally canonized by the Church in 1920, and her feast day is celebrated on May 30.

Mission

The youngest of five children, Joan drew her mission in life from her parents' example of faith. From her earliest years, Joan was known for her generosity, goodness, kindness, obedience, and religious devotion. Others who lived near Joan remembered her tender ministries when she nursed a friend back to health or when she gave up her bed for a homeless stranger. They reported that she was often teased for being too pious. Joan's good heart and strong faith allowed her to listen obediently to the voices that urged her to boldly undertake what seemed an impossible task. Although she was young, female, and untrained as a military leader, Joan accepted God's direction for her life. She bravely faced those in authority and convinced them of her sincere purpose. As a result of her willingness to follow in faith, she single-handedly rallied a nation and saved her country.

Legacy

Joan of Arc is the patron saint of France; however, her life inspires faith throughout the Christian world. Her legacy is not one of blind patriotism or nationalism, but rather one of faithful obedience to God's call on our lives. Joan serves as a witness that we can undertake the impossible and triumph if we trust ourselves completely to God's care. Her life reminds us that, although others may discount us as too young or untried, God sees our potential. Saint Joan's legacy is the reality that God can bring about mighty works through the lives of those who are open to the prompting of the Spirit.

Bodily/Kinesthetic Intelligence

Learn

By dramatizing Joan of Arc's story with body puppets, participants will explore the Saint's relationships with people and enact significant events in her life.

Locate

Resources on the life of Saint Joan of Arc; Grocery bags, brown paper; Construction paper; Glue; Markers; Plastic bags; Rubber bands; Scissors; Stapler; Staples; Yarn.

Lead

Although Joan of Arc is the person whose life is remembered and celebrated, many people influenced and shaped the impact that this saint made on the political and religious history of the world. Discuss with the participants the important roles that others play in our lives. Ask the participants to name people who helped to shape the life of Saint Joan. If the learners have studied the life of the saint, ask them to brainstorm a list of people who played a role in Joan's life and some of the major turning points that they can identify. Suggest ones they may overlook and guide them to organize their list chronologically. If the students are just learning the facts related to Saint Joan, then divide the class into small groups and assign them to read about the following periods in her life and to record significant influences provided by people and events. Categories might include:

A Simple Childhood
    Father and Mother
    Brothers and Sister

A Call from God
    Parish Priest
    Voices of Saint Catherine of Alexandria, Saint Margaret of Antioch, and Saint Michael the
        Archangel

A Girl Meets a King
    Robert deBaudricourt
    Dauphin/King Charles VII
    Board of Theologians

A Young Lady Becomes a Soldier
    French Army

A Hero Is Betrayed
    Bishop Peter Cauchon of Beauvais
    Duke of Burgundy
    King Henry VI of England
    Court at Trial

A Martyr Becomes a Saint
    Witnesses to her Martyrdom
    Participants in Re-trial
    Pope Benedict XV

Once the information is gathered, explain to the students that they will make body puppets to represent the people involved in the story of Saint Joan's life. Invite individuals, partners, or groups to select two or three categories to dramatize. From their chosen category, have each student select one influential person to depict.

Demonstrate the process for constructing a body puppet, a type of puppet that is worn—rather than held—to operate it. Select a character to create, perhaps Saint Joan of Arc. Start with a full size brown paper grocery bag. The bottom flap of the bag will become the puppet's head and the remainder of the bag will be the body. Choose a full sheet of construction paper and glue it to the body portion of the bag. Make a face on the flap. Decorate the character with marker and additional construction paper.

Make a neck strap by cutting a 30" length of yarn. Staple the center of the yarn to the middle of the top of the bag. For arms, cut two 2" x 18" strips of plastic bag. Tie a rubber band to the end of each piece of plastic. Staple the other end of each arm strip to the plastic bag, just below the flap.

To wear and work the puppet, tie the yarn around the neck, and slip the rubber bands over the wrists. The puppeteer's motions and movements manipulate the character.

Provide supplies for the project and guide the group as they create a variety of body puppets to represent the people that were influential in the life of Saint Joan of Arc.

Once the puppets are completed, use them as characters in telling "The Life of Saint Joan of Arc." Based on their reading and discussion, have the participants improvise the story line for each scenario. Once the class has enjoyed creating their puppet plays, invite them to perform for other groups or for a special program.

Interpersonal Intelligence

Learn

By participating in literary circles, learners will work together to discuss, record, and share ideas related to books and movies based on the life of Saint Joan of Arc.

Locate

Books on the life of Saint Joan of Arc; Movies about Saint Joan; Paper; Pencils or pens; VCR and Monitor.

Lead

Joan of Arc, the Maid of Orleans—also known as Jeanne la Pucelle—was born at Domremy, France in 1412 and died at Rouen in 1431. She was declared a saint in 1920, not for her patriotism to her country or her military valor, but for the virtue of her life and her faithfulness to God. Saint Joan of Arc's feast day is commemorated on May 30. There are many books and movies—as well as pieces of music and works of art—devoted to the life of Saint Joan. Varied interpretations exist to present historical information about this celebrated saint. Based on the ages and the interests of the group, select a sampling of resources from community, parish or school libraries and video sources for the students to use in small groups known as "literary circles". Suggestions include:

Primary Grades

Books

Dove and Sword: A Novel of Joan of Arc. Garden, Nancy. New York: Scholastic, 1997.

Joan of Arc. Poole, Josephine and Angela Barrett. New York: Knopf, 1998.

Joan of Arc. Stanley, Diane. New York: Morrow, 1998.

Joan of Arc: The Lily Maid. Hodges, Margaret and Robert Rayevsky, Illustrator. New York: Holiday House, 1999.

Movies

Joan of Arc. Nest Entertainment, Inc. Animated Hero Classics, 1996. 30 Minutes

Wishbone's Bone of Arc. Wishbone Series, 1995

Intermediate Grades

Books

Beyond The Myth: The Story of Joan of Arc. Brooks, Polly Schoyer. Boston, MA: Houghton Mifflin, 1999.

Joan of Arc. Twain, Mark with Jean Francois Alden, Translator. Ft. Collins, CO: Ignatius Press, 1990.

Joan of Arc: By Herself and Her Witnesses. Pernoud, Regine. Lanham, MD: Scarborough House, 1994.

Personal Recollections of Joan Of Arc. Twain, Mark and Robert Raven. Princeton, NJ: Xlibris Corporation, 2000.

Movies

Joan of Arc. Artisan Entertainment. Maid of Orleans Productions, Inc., an Alliance Atlantis Company, 1999. 140 Minutes.

Saint Joan. (with Otto Preminger and Jean Seberg, 1956)

Using a variety of biographies and movies based on the life of Saint Joan, create literary circles to involve the students in the discussion of these books and films. If several class periods are available, set aside at least one session to organize the project, to select resources, and to assign roles for the groups to discuss. Allow time, preferably out of class, for group members to read the books and to view the films. Devote another session to discussion of the reading/viewing and one or more periods for groups to share their findings. If only one session is available for the entire activity, show a film clip or read a selection from a book and assign groups to create their presentations in class based on what they viewed or heard.

Regardless of the format, begin by organizing the learners into small groups, with each group selecting one title as their focus for study. Assign group members individual roles to play as their team reads or views the selection. Roles should include:

Discussion Leader
A person who writes questions for the group to guide their conversation.

Group Facilitator
Student who takes notes, keeps the team on task, and reports group findings to the class.

Illustrator
Someone who designs or draws significant scenes from parts of the book or movie.

Word Wizard
Individual who collects new vocabulary words or important quotes found in the text.

If possible, reading and viewing should be done outside of class. This may require locating several copies of each book, or arranging a "screening" session of the movies. Agree upon a timeline for completing the reading or viewing assignment.

Once the assignment is completed, students should come prepared to discuss in their groups what they understood, found important, or were surprised to learn. The discussion leader should bring several questions that get the group talking; for example, "What is one new idea about Saint Joan that this book (or movie) gave you?" Or, the discussion leader may use a teacher prepared list as a springboard for conversation. The illustrator should bring two or three drawings or images of significant scenes. These may also be sketched in class. The word wizard should bring any special vocabulary definitions or important quotes. These, too, may be recorded during discussion. The facilitator should take responsibility for keeping the conversation on task and jotting down the main ideas voiced. This will help him or her plan a presentation for the entire class.

Instruct each group to prepare a review to share with the rest of the class. They should offer a brief summary of their findings, share pictures or images that communicate significant scenes from the story, and present a vocabulary and/or quote list. They should also offer a "thumbs up" or "thumbs down" critique and explain why they think others would or would not benefit from reading or viewing this story of Saint Joan of Arc.

Intrapersonal Intelligence

Learn

By creating a personal crest, participants will focus on their important values for life, like those depicted on the crest of Saint Joan of Arc.

Locate

Cardboard or poster board; Construction paper; Crayons or Markers; Glue; Hole punch; Magazines; Paper; Pattern for crest; Pencils; Photograph of each student (Optional); Scissors.

Lead

Because of her remarkable accomplishments, Joan of Arc and her family were granted a place in the nobility by King Charles VII of France. This meant that they were entitled to a special crest that distinguished their family, identifying members of their household and any of their descendants. The crest was a sword surmounted by a crown on a field of blue, with a *fleur-de-lis* on each side of the sword. The *fleur-de-lis* had both national and religious significance. The ancient *fleur-de-lis* was the emblem of the French royal family, with the three leaves symbolizing faith, valor, and wisdom. Religiously the *fleur-de-lis* or iris was the symbol of the Trinity because of the three-in-one nature of the blossom. Thus, Joan of Arc was reminded by the crest's design of her loyalty to her king and her faith in the triune God.

After sharing the story of Saint Joan's crest, explaining the symbolism, and if possible, showing an illustration or a picture of it, inform the participants that they will design a crest of their own. Explain that the crest was often found on a shield as a "coat of arms," a symbol associated with protection. However, the crest is also used as an emblem simply to depict personal traits of an individual.

Invite the students to think about the unique qualities that God has given to each of them. Using paper and pencil, tell each person in the group to list and describe several of their gifts. These ideas will become part of a personal crest or shield.

Provide patterns for the crest, cardboard (or poster board), pencils, and scissors. Direct each pupil to trace the crest pattern onto the heavy material and to cut out the shape. Place additional supplies within sharing distance of the students. Suggest that they cut a large cross from construction paper and glue it to the center of the crest. If pictures of each participant are available, glue one to the center of each crest. As an alternative to using an actual photograph, tell the learners to draw a self-portrait and attach it to the shield shape. Next, direct the pupils to draw, color, cut, and glue pictures that highlight their abilities, interests, and talents to the sections of the crest. If desired, punch holes in the top of the crest and tie a length of ribbon through them to serve as a hanger.

Display the crests and celebrate the gifts that God has given each person and the ways in which they are used to serve God.

Logical/Mathematical Intelligence

Learn

By compiling a timeline, participants will put into perspective significant dates from the life of Saint Joan of Arc.

Locate

Biography of Joan of Arc; Construction paper; Markers; Masking tape or push pins.

Lead

A timeline provides a way to put the events of history in order—to actually visualize what happened at what point in time. Because the Christian world uses the birth of Jesus to divide and date history, abbreviations in a timeline often include BC, BCE, and A.D.. BC stands for before Christ, BCE refers to before the Common Era or before the Christian Era, and A.D., the Latin words *Anno Domini*, mean "in the year of our Lord." The letter c., an abbreviation for circa, before a date means about or around that year. It is important to note that dates vary depending on the reference materials used to compile a timeline. It is helpful to consult several sources to verify information.

Review significant dates from a biography on Joan of Arc. Then create a timeline to help the students remember the sequence of events that occurred during the life of this saint. Dates could include:

January 6, 1412—Joan of Arc is born at Domremy, France

Midsummer, 1424—Joan first hears voices

May, 1428—Joan goes to Vaucouleurs

February, 1429—Joan leaves for Chinon

March 9, 1429—Joan meets with Charles VII

Early March—March 21, 1429—Joan is examined by the theologians at Poitiers

May 8, 1429—Joan liberates Orleans

July 17, 1429—Joan attends the coronation of Charles VII at Rheims

December 29, 1429—Joan is ennobled along with her family, given a coat of arms, and the surname "de Lys"

March/April, 1430—Joan conquers Compiegne

May 23, 1430—Joan is captured

May-November, 1430—Joan is imprisoned at Beaulieu and Beaurevoir

November/December, 1430—Joan is moved to Rouen

January 3, 1431—Joan is transferred to the custody of Bishop Cauchon

January 9, 1431—Joan's "Trial of Condemnation" begins

May 28/29, 1431—Joan is proclaimed a relapsed heretic and abandoned to secular authorities

May 30, 1431—Joan is burned alive on Rouen's old market square

1450—Joan's "Trial of Rehabilitation" begins

1456—Joan is exonerated of guilt

1920—Joan is canonized a saint

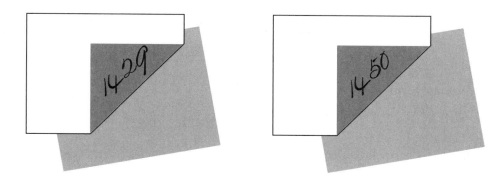

After discussing the significance of the events that took place at various times throughout Joan of Arc's life, choose eight to ten dates to highlight in a timeline. Individually, or in small groups, instruct the students to select eight to ten pieces of construction paper—the same or different colors. Use each sheet to tell part of the story of the events that are recorded in the history of Saint Joan. Write each date only on the backs of the pages.

Individually, in small groups, or as a class, shuffle the papers and try to put the events in sequence. Select one sheet at a time and tack or tape it to a bulletin board, table, or wall in the order in which the events occurred in the life of Saint Joan of Arc. Use the dates on the back to check the order as the group is working.

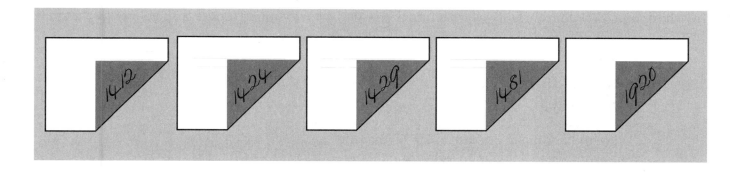

Musical/Rhythmic Intelligence

Learn

By writing a ballad telling the story of Saint Joan of Arc, participants will use rhyme and rhythm to remember significant events and words from her life.

Locate

Chalkboard and chalk or newsprint and markers; Paper; Pencils or pens; Resource materials on the life of Saint Joan of Arc.

Lead

A ballad is a long poem or song that tells a story in short stanzas, usually quatrains, and simple words, often with a refrain or a chorus. Quatrains are four-line poems that follow any of these four different rhyme patterns:

AABB

ABAB

ABBA

ABCB

When quatrains are combined to form longer poems, each group of four lines is called a stanza. Stanzas are the paragraphs of poetry. Quatrains are used in ballads to tell a tale, most often a sad story. Involve the class in a group project to write a ballad about the life of Saint Joan of Arc.

Prior to the activity, lead the participants in a review of the highlights of Joan's life. Be sure to include her childhood, her call from God, her meeting with Charles to volunteer for the war, her battles, her participation in Charles' coronation, her capture, and her death.

Begin the project by sharing the stanzas of the sample ballad with the group.

Joan's Childhood

Formula: ABCB

In childhood, Saint Joan heard the voices of saints

Who told her that God had a plan for her life

She would lead soldiers to fight for her land

With God at her side they would win o'er the strife.

Joan's Death

Formula: AABB

In time, Joan could see that her life would soon end

Despite all her vict'ries, no one spoke as her friend.

Tied to the stake Joan seemed to have lost,

But she triumphed again as she gazed at the cross.

After reading these or other stanzas to the participants, invite them to write quatrains as a method of learning more of the history of Saint Joan of Arc. Print the poetry patterns—AABB, ABAB, ABBA, and ABCB—on a chalkboard or on newsprint so the students may refer to the formulas. Point out the resource materials available for the students' use. Distribute newsprint sheets and markers to each person or group. Guide the learners as they locate and list information about the story of Joan of Arc. If the group is large, assign a different portion of her life to each person or cluster and compile information about her biography by combining the stanzas. As another option, suggest that the students adapt or include some of Joan of Arc's notable quotations and incorporate them into their verses. For example:

Joan at Vaucouleurs: Asked about her mission, she replied: "I was born for this." Asked if she was afraid, she answered: "I fear nothing for God is with me."

Joan at Chinon: Joan's greeting to Charles: "Gentle Dauphin, my name is Joan, the Maid. The King of Heaven has sent me to bring you and your kingdom help."

Joan at Poitiers: Asked if she believed in God: "Indeed, yes, better than you do!" Joan's motto: "It is God Who commands it!"

Joan at Orleans: Joan's reply to Dunois of Orleans: "I bring you better help than has ever come to any general or town, for the help I bring comes from the King of Heaven."
Joan's refusal to use a charm to heal her wound: "No friend, I cannot. I would rather die than do a thing which I know to be a sin."

Joan's Reply to the Church Leaders of Rouen
Asked if she was in God's grace: "If I am not, may God put me there, and if I am, may God so keep me! I should be the saddest creature in the world if I knew I was not in his grace."
"Everything I have said or done is in the hands of God. I commit myself to him! I certify to you that I would do or say nothing against the Christian faith."

Joan Is Informed of her Impending Death
Joan's reply to Bishop Cauchon: "Bishop, I die because of you!"
Joan's response to the Bishop's denial of guilt: "If you had placed me in the Church's prison and gave me into the hands of competent and suitable Church guardians, this would not have happened. That is why I appeal to God for justice against you!"

Joan's Last Words
"Hold the crucifix up before my eyes so I may see it until I die."
"My voices did come from God and everything that I have done was by God's order."
Once the stanzas are completed, post the newsprint sheets around the room and read the verses together.

Naturalist Intelligence

Learn

By blending images of creation with verses from the Psalms, participants will be reminded to take strength in God from nature, as Saint Joan of Arc once did.

Locate

Bibles; Calendars with nature photographs; Film; Glue or tape; Magazines; Markers, pencils or pens; Paper; Polaroid cameras; Scissors.

Lead

Reflecting upon the life of Saint Joan of Arc inspires us to recognize that she took her strength entirely from her faith in God. Joan looked upon God as the light to guide her steps and as the rock of her faith, her stronghold in times of trouble. The Psalms abound with images of God as our salvation. Psalm 27 is especially appropriate to the life of this woman of faith. In this Psalm David celebrates God as "my light and my salvation." Even though he must face "false witnesses" who are "breathing out violence," he will not fear, but will "wait for the Lord." Certainly these words would have been familiar to Saint Joan and would have comforted her in her own time of trouble.

Read Psalm 27 aloud in unison, as a responsive reading—alternating verses between individuals or groups, or as a choral reading—assigning separate voices to different phrases. Discuss the Psalm's image of God as light. Ask what pictures come to mind when thinking about God as light, for example, the sun, moon, and stars of the heavens. Invite the participants to picture the power of the God who can set us "high on a rock." Explain that these words from Scripture and images from nature would have been familiar ones to Saint Joan. Explain that David, who wrote many of the Psalms, took inspiration from the world around him.

Ask the students to select words from the Psalm that they find particularly meaningful or comforting. Invite them to close their eyes and to imagine scenes from nature that would illustrate these words. Challenge them to connect the beauty of nature and the words of Scripture through photography. Give instructions either for using cameras to take pictures of nature or for choosing pictures of nature cut from old magazines or outdated calendars. Provide additional supplies, such as paper, markers, pencils or pens, scissors, and glue or tape, for the project. Guide the learners as they take or find photos to illustrate words, as well as phrases, from the verses of Psalm 27.

Invite the students to share their images and to connect them to the lines from Psalm 27. Have them read the verses aloud as they hold up their pictures. Create a composite collage on a bulletin board or a large piece of paper using the photos that the students provide and the passages from Psalm 27. Remind everyone to take strength from nature as a reminder of the constant presence of God.

Verbal/Linguistic Intelligence

Learn

By experiencing a first-person narrative, participants will comprehend biographical information regarding Saint Joan of Arc and connect the events of her life to a related Bible story, 1 Samuel 3, and to the importance of responding to God's call.

Locate

Bible; Costume for "Sexton"; Story script.

Lead

Share the story of Saint Joan of Arc and tell the related Bible story as a first-person narrative. To enhance learning and to make the story memorable, a costumed "Sexton" should relate memories about his favorite saint, Joan of Arc.

"Sexton" Story Script
(adapted from: 1 Samuel 3)

Bon jour! My name is Marcel; in English, you would call me "little Mark." I know that I am not very big, but I have an important job! I am the sexton at our little village church here in Domremy. That means I ring the bell when it is time for the Mass, when it is time for prayers, when someone is married, or when, sadly, someone dies. Others might think that my job does not matter, but I believe God has given me this ministry of the bells as my calling! When I hear the sound ring out pure and clear, calling people to church and to prayer, I hear the very voice of God.

Someone from my village taught me how to listen for the voice of God. Her name was Joan, Jeanne we called her when she was a little girl. She was always a special child, faithful to come and pray here at the church. She was always kind to me, not ignoring me as many folks seemed to do. She once told me that she liked to hear the bells when she was out tending her family's sheep in the pasture. Their sound was like the voice of God to her, too. Joan told me that she often heard the voices of the saints as well. I believed her. She was so sincere and had such a good heart. She confided in me that the voices told her that she would help free France and return the rightful king to the throne. I was not surprised when she was able to accomplish that very thing! Imagine: someone from our small village called by God to such a mighty work!

Others might have scoffed, but that is because they don't know God. When Joan told me about the voices she heard, I reminded her of the Old Testament story of Samuel. As a young boy, he heard the voice of God calling him to be a prophet. At first he didn't understand, but then Eli the priest told him to say, "Speak, Lord, your servant is listening." Samuel grew to be a great prophet, even anointing God's chosen King David when he was but a young boy. So Samuel anointed the king who saved his people, and David's descendant, Jesus, saved the world. You see how God's purpose is accomplished when people follow in faith. I encouraged Joan to listen to God's message for her, as well. When Joan listened to the voices she heard, she was able to save France. Her voice was like a clear bell, calling the faithful to have purpose and fear not.

God does not call all of us to mighty tasks, but we are all called by God to some duty. You may say that you do not hear the voice of God, but I say to you, listen! I hear the voice of God in the sound of the bell. Though I am small, when I ring the bells, I am doing God's work. You, too, must be willing to listen for God's voice. You, too, will have a mission. Like Joan, you must trust God's call on your life and respond in faith and love. Who knows what you might accomplish? God does!

Visual/Spatial Intelligence

Learn

By designing a personal pennant, participants will understand the nature of Joan of Arc's allegiance to God and consider their own commitment as well.

Locate

Dowel rods or long drinking straws; Felt; Glue or tape; Paper; Pencils; Permanent markers; Pictures of Saint Joan of Arc's flag(s); Rulers; Scissors.

Advance Preparation

Cut felt into 9" x 12" pieces, one per participant.

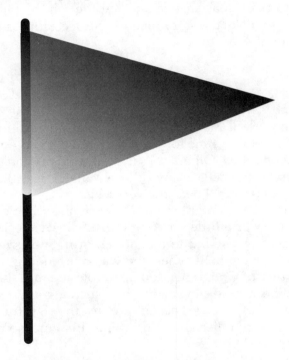

Lead

During her leadership of the Army of France, Joan of Arc had three special types of flags designed for her—a banner, a pennon, and a standard. Joan's three-feet-wide and twelve-feet-long standard was made of buckram, a material similar to an artist's canvas, and had a silken fringe. This "fluttering sign" served as a symbol and a rallying point for the soldiers on a field of battle. On a background of golden lilies, an image of the King of Heaven sat upon a rainbow, holding the world in one hand and raising the other hand in benediction. Before him, to the right and to the left, were the kneeling figures of Michael and Gabriel, each presenting God with a *fleur-de-lis*. The motto "Jesus-Mary" was written in letters of gold. The reverse side was an azure blue color, sporting a silver dove that held a streamer in its beak.

Discuss the symbols on Saint Joan's standard and the priorities they might suggest for Joan and her troops. For example, the image of God as the King of Heaven blessing the *fleur-de-lis* conveys that Joan was asking God's blessing on her country, France. Her motto of "Jesus-Mary" served to remind the troops of their Christian faith and their commitment to God. Help the learners understand that the purpose of the standard was to serve as a rallying point when the confusion of battle might separate the soldiers. The flag also served as a reminder of their purpose and gave them courage to keep fighting.

Explain to the participants that they will design their own pennant as a reminder of Saint Joan's battle flag. Invite the students to consider symbols and words that could represent their commitment to God and their mission in life. Discuss symbols to use on a standard such as a cross to symbolize Jesus or a *fleur-de-lis* to represent the Trinity. Talk about words to use as a motto. Offer ideas such as faith, hope, and love. Challenge the group to create personal pennants to declare these messages.

Demonstrate the process for the pupils. Choose a 9" x 12" piece of felt. With a ruler and a pencil, measure along one 9" side and mark the center point at 4 1/2". To form a triangular pennant shape, draw lines from the center mark on one end of the paper to both corners along the opposite edge. Cut out the triangle and set it aside. Select a piece of paper and a pencil. Draw or write different arrangements of symbols and words on the sheet. Then, using permanent markers, copy the design onto the triangle of felt. Glue a dowel rod or a long drinking straw directly to the felt along the short end of the triangle. Or, fold and glue the edge to form a casing and slide the dowel or straw through the tube.

Provide supplies for the project and guide the participants as they prepare their personal pennants. When everyone has completed a flag, display the pennants and share excitement about each person's commitment to God.

JUNE
SAINT PETER

Biography

Simon, later called Peter by Jesus, was a fisherman of Capernaum (Mark 1:30) or Bethsaida (John 1:44). He was married, and his wife, whose mother Jesus healed, may have accompanied him on his missionary journeys (1 Corinthians 9:5).

The gospels are unanimous in describing him as one of the first disciples and the leader of the apostles. He was present at most of the chief incidents in Jesus' life and, with the sons of Zebedee, formed Jesus' inner circle.

He is best remembered for two acts: his recognition of Jesus as Messiah at Caesarea Philippi and his denial of Jesus at the crucifixion. After the first, Jesus bestowed the name Peter on him: "Thou art Peter and upon this rock will I build my church" (Matthew 14:17-19). After the denial, Peter fled, probably home to Galilee to resume fishing.

Later, after Pentecost, Peter became the recognized leader of the Apostles and spent the rest of his life teaching, preaching, healing, and doing missionary work. He is said to have been the first bishop of Antioch and served as the first bishop of Rome—and hence the first pope. He was crucified in Rome under Nero around A.D. 64. At his own request, Peter died with his head down.

Saint Peter's feast day, which he shares with another great apostle, Saint Paul, is June 29.

Mission

Even though he had betrayed his Lord, Peter went on to baptize many, including Cornelius, the first Gentile admitted into the church. He healed the sick and lame, raised the dead, and performed many kind acts—while preaching the Good News of Jesus. For this, he was frequently thrown into prison or otherwise punished. His story appears in the gospels and Acts.

Legacy

As one of the first disciples, Peter eagerly answered Jesus' call, left his fishing nets, and followed Jesus during his ministry. It was Peter who first identified Jesus as the Messiah, or "the Christ, the Son of the Living God." And it was Peter who first led the Christian church and died for it as an early martyr. Even though he denied Jesus at the time of the crucifixion, he spent the rest of his life serving the church. He was the first pope. Finally, he sacrificed his life for his Lord, being hung on a cross upside-down in humble deference to the way the Lord was crucified.

Bodily/Kinesthetic Intelligence

Learn

By retelling a Bible story, Matthew 14:22-33, participants will understand the importance that Jesus, as well as Saint Peter, placed on being a faithful follower of God.

Locate

"Peter Walks On Water" Rhythm Story Script.

Lead

As an engaging method of teaching Jesus' followers today about Saint Peter's lesson in faith, invite everyone to share in retelling the Bible story of Peter walking on water by clapping a rhythm and echoing a rhyme. Explain that in a rhythm story the leader says a line and the participants repeat it. Begin by establishing the clapping pattern, one clap on the knees followed by one clap of the hands, and practice it several times. Chant the first line of the story to this rhythm and tell the group to echo it back. Communicate the entire message in this manner. Maintain the established rhythm throughout the activity.

"Peter Walks on Water" Rhythm Story
(Scripture: Matthew 14:22-33)

Simon was a fisherman
And a loud, outspoken guy.
But he left his net, his boat, his
Fish, when Jesus happened by.

"Come follow me," said Jesus.
"I'll even change your name."
"You'll be my rock of faith" he said.
Peter never was the same.

Peter learned to fish for people.
He stayed close by Jesus' side.
"My faith in you," said Peter
"Can never be denied."

"I can even walk on water.
Watch and tell me what you think!"
But he took his eyes off Jesus
"Master, help me or I'll sink!"

No Peter wasn't perfect.
He was just like you and me.
But Jesus looked past Peter's
Faults and saw who he could be.

So, when we follow Jesus
Though we might not change our names
We will learn to fish for people.
And we'll never be the same.

Interpersonal Intelligence

Learn

By viewing structures or by observing elements of architecture, learners will work together through the format of a scavenger hunt to learn about Peter's life.

Locate

Books and encyclopedias featuring works of architecture, art, sculpture or stained glass; Duplicating equipment; List of nearby places bearing Saint Peter's name; Paper; Pens; Pictures of various symbols used to represent Peter; Resources such as slides or photos of famous sites related to Peter; Scavenger hunt sheets.

Advance Preparation

Make necessary arrangements for field trips, speakers, audio-visuals and equipment. Prepare "Scavenger Hunt" sheets and duplicate a copy for each participant.

Lead

Many churches have been built and works of art have been created to honor Peter, the first pope. Design an architectural "scavenger hunt" to help participants learn about the mission and ministry of this great saint. Regardless of the format for the scavenger hunt, participants can be divided into teams, then given the same number of questions to research and the same amount of time to find the answers.

Explore the local community to find churches or other architecture dedicated to the Apostle Peter. Plan field trips to any church of Saint Peter in the area or to other sites commemorating the disciple. Learn as much as possible about the history of any structure or embellishment connected with Saint Peter. Design a "scavenger hunt" to find answers to the following questions:

Is the artist or architect still available?

Who were the members of the original planning committee?

Why was the name or symbolism for Peter significant to the planners?

Is the theme of Saint Peter evident in more than one place in the building?

What are documents or records explaining the art work?

What Biblical passage is connected with the artwork?

Name a fact you can learn from news articles about building plans, dedication, or anniversary celebrations?

Challenge the group or individuals to research and to record any information that is discovered. Get permission from building owners or church administrators to take photographs, to make sketches, or to do rubbings of any visual representations of Saint Peter. Present the data in a booklet or as a talk.

Another kind of scavenger hunt would be to explore art galleries, museums, and libraries to learn more about the life of Peter. Challenge the teams to find examples of various types of architecture and art related to Saint Peter, for example: carving, painting, sculpture, stained glass, and so forth. Take time to present the information to the entire group.

For an in-class activity, invite speakers and provide reference materials to learn about famous architecture bearing the name of the Apostle Peter. Find information in travel materials, public libraries, museums, and on the Internet. The most notable church is Saint Peter's Basilica in Rome. It is thought to be the world's largest Catholic church and is the seat of the Church. Two churches, both called Saint

Peter's, have been built over what is believed to be Peter's burial site. The first one, built about 325, was torn down in 1506, and construction of the present building took nearly 150 years to complete. The basic floor plan of the Basilica is in the shape of a Latin cross.

Design an in-class scavenger hunt sheet with questions on this church of St. Peter's in Rome such as:

- What other interesting facts are there about this important church? (world's largest Christian church)
- What is the name of the most famous chapel which is part of the church? (Sistine Chapel)
- Who was the renowned artist who painted the ceiling in the chapel and engineered the large dome? (Michelangelo)
- Who are some of the other men considered to be the architects and interior designers? (Bernini, Bramante)
- What great leader commissioned the building of the first church to symbolize his acceptance of Christianity? (Constantine)
- Who decided to rebuild the church? (Pope Nicholas V)
- What facts are recorded about measurements of the huge structure? (basic floor plan is in shape of Latin cross)

After researching the setting, decor and history that make this a fascinating monument to Saint Peter, allow an opportunity for sharing information.

Intrapersonal Intelligence

Learn

By using imaginative reflection, learners will discover their own personal answers to questions Jesus asked of Saint Peter.

Locate

Bibles; Paper; Pencils; Script.

Lead

Like any good teacher, Jesus guided his pupils with critical questions that made them think and develop important skills. Reading any gospel account will reveal numerous questions Jesus presented to his disciples, many directed to Peter specifically. Use the script provided to guide your own thinking or to lead a group in experiencing Christ's final question to Peter. If possible, play quiet background music or nature sounds like that of wind or surf.

Guided Mediation Script

Before beginning an imaginative recreation of scripture, be sure to take time to clear your mind and prayerfully focus your thoughts. Sit comfortably in your chair. Rest your feet on the floor and allow your body to relax. Feel the chair supporting you as you choose to sit quietly and experience a time of reflection.

Breathe in deeply through your nose and exhale slowly through your mouth. Take three of these deep cleansing breaths, and then simply listen to the sound of your breathing as you sink further into rest and relaxation. Feel your feet and legs begin to relax, and allow that feeling to travel up your body. Let your hands and wrists go limp. Circle your shoulders and release the tension in your neck and back. As you breathe slowly and naturally, imagine that you breathe in God's peace and holy presence and exhale doubt and worry.

In the now quiet space of your mind, imagine that you are at the seashore at dawn. Hear the cry of the sea birds; smell the fresh breeze coming inland over the water. See the light begin on the distant horizon and watch as the sky transforms in radiant shades of blue, pink, and gold. Feel the damp coolness of the sand under your feet as you begin to walk along the shore. Occasionally, the incoming tide splashes you with the advancing waves. You find the cold sensation invigorating. Every fiber of your being seems alive to the experience.

In the distance, you see a figure cooking breakfast over an outdoor fire. You plan to walk past the stranger, but as you approach, he gestures for you to come and join him. He speaks your name, and you turn to look directly into his face. You recognize him as Jesus. He is smiling at you, and he invites you by name to share his meal. See him reaching his hand out to you. See yourself accepting his invitation and joining him at the fire.

He shares what he is cooking with you, but first he lifts his eyes to heaven in blessing. Your heart joins his as he praises God's goodness. You listen carefully as he prays. How does he bless the food? How does he bless you?

What do you talk about as you share this meal together? What concerns do you speak about with him? His eyes speak care and concern as he listens to you. Now Jesus would talk with you. He bids you to follow him, and you walk along the shore together.

Jesus turns to you and asks, "Do you love me?" Hear yourself respond. A little farther on, Jesus asks again, "Do you love me?" How can you speak your answer with more conviction? Answer him again.

Feel the intensity as Jesus asks you a third time, "Do you love me?" What are your emotions? What more do you need to say? Respond with your whole heart.

Jesus now gives you instructions about what you are to do with your life. What are you to do? How are you to live? You will never forget this moment as you are commissioned by Christ to offer your gifts to his people.

You return with Jesus to the campfire. He offers you a token to bring with you as a reminder of your time together. What gift does he give you? You understand that you are to return to the present moment with new courage and resolve. You reluctantly say goodbye and begin the journey back along the shore. You turn once and wave, and Jesus waves back to you.

You know that somehow he is always here waiting for you when you need him. As you walk along the beach, you become aware of the sound of your own breathing. Allow that sound to bring you back to the present moment, to the sounds and objects in this room. When you are ready, you may open your eyes and create some record of the memories of this experience.

If appropriate, offer paper and pens and allow time for participants to reflect on the experience.

Logical/Mathematical Intelligence

Learn

By using numbers as answers to a crossword puzzle, participants will learn facts about Peter's life.

Locate

Bibles; Saint Peter Crossword Puzzle; Duplicating equipment; Paper; Pencils.

Advance Preparation

Duplicate Saint Peter Crossword Puzzle.

Lead

One. Two. Three. Fifty. Three thousand. Many numbers come to mind when one thinks about the life of Simon Peter. As number one, he and his brother Andrew were the first disciples to be called to follow Jesus. During the course of his ministry, Jesus gave Simon a second name, Peter, for a special reason. Peter's words, recorded in Matthew 16:16, Mark 8:29, and Luke 9:20, form the basis for the creeds and confessions of the church today. Three times Peter denied Jesus and three times Peter was assured of Jesus' love and forgiveness. Fifty days after Jesus' resurrection, on the day of Pentecost, Peter was filled with the Holy Spirit and preached a powerful sermon, resulting in the conversion of at least 3,000 new believers.

These numbers, and others, form the structure for clues in a crossword puzzle about Peter. Use the project to help participants learn more about the countless ways in which Peter's ministry and mission influenced the early church and the church today. Distribute a copy of the crossword puzzle and a pencil to each student. Offer Bibles for those who need additional help. Review the answers following the activity.

Answers

ACROSS	DOWN
1. Two	2. one
4. twelve	3. four
6. sixteen	4. Three Thousand
7. Six	5. fifty
8. three	

Saint Peter Crossword Puzzle

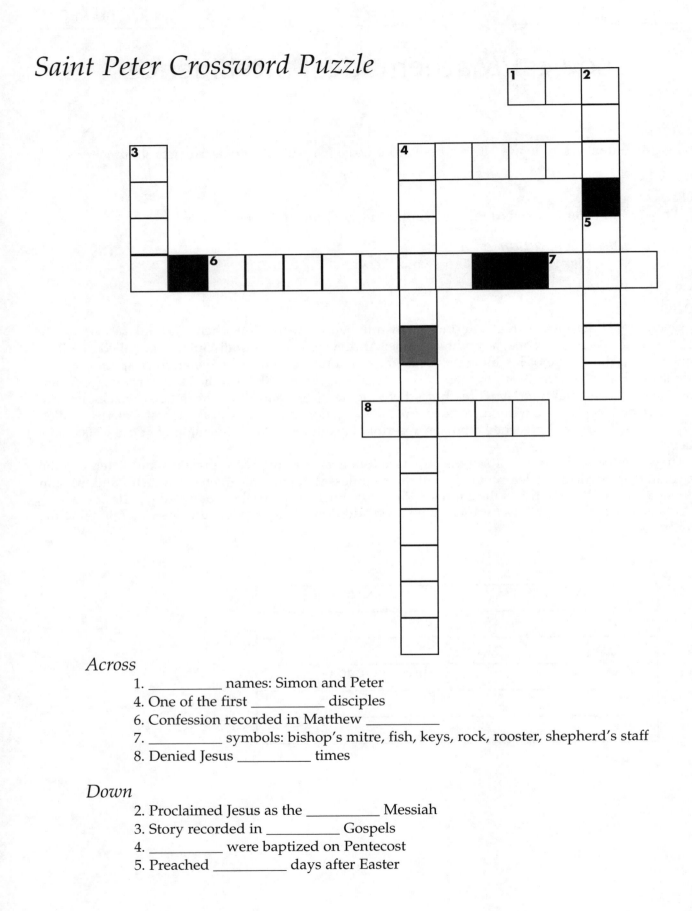

Across

1. _____ names: Simon and Peter
4. One of the first _____ disciples
6. Confession recorded in Matthew _____
7. _____ symbols: bishop's mitre, fish, keys, rock, rooster, shepherd's staff
8. Denied Jesus _____ times

Down

2. Proclaimed Jesus as the _____ Messiah
3. Story recorded in _____ Gospels
4. _____ were baptized on Pentecost
5. Preached _____ days after Easter

Musical/Rhythmic Intelligence

Learn
By using music as a teaching tool, participants will address the topics and themes of Peter's life.

Locate
Accompaniment (Optional); Bibles; Hymnals; Music for selected songs; Paper; Pens.

Lead
Tell the story of Peter's life or teach a theme related to his legacy through music. Write new words to an existing tune and sing the scripture.

Compose new words to the song "Michael, Row The Boat Ashore." Sing the first verse of the song together to be sure everyone knows the tune. Then create new verses based on the Bible stories and themes related to Peter's life. Start with these sample verses and make up more. Be sure to repeat each phrase four times.

> Jesus said, "Come, Follow Me." Alleluia.
> Jesus calmed the angry sea. Alleluia.
> Jesus rose up from the grave. Alleluia.
> Jesus told me, "Feed My Sheep." Alleluia.

As an additional or alternate activity, use music to highlight the key events of Peter's life. Compile a list of six to ten scripture passages that tell Peter's story in chronological order. Then using a hymnal, find a song that communicates each theme. For example:

Peter is called by Jesus—Matthew 4:18-22
    "Jesus Calls Us" (words: Cecil Francis Alexander, music: William H. Jude)

Peter witnesses Jesus' miracles and ministry—Matthew 8:14-17
    "Thine Arm, O Lord, In Days Of Old" (Edward H. Plumptree)

Peter confesses Jesus as the Messiah—Matthew 16:13-20
    "Fairest Lord Jesus" (Silesian folk melody)

Peter denies Jesus—Matthew 26:69-75
    "In The Hour Of Trial" (James Montgomery)

Peter is present at the crucifixion—Matthew 26:32-56
    "Were You There?" (African-American spiritual)

Peter is an eyewitness to the resurrection—John 20:2-10
    "Up from the Grave He Arose" (Robert Lowry)

Peter is commissioned by Jesus—John 21:1-22
    "My Jesus, I Love Thee" (words: William R. Featherstone, music: Adoniram J. Gordan)

Peter is filled with the Holy Spirit on Pentecost—Acts 2:13-42
   "O For A Thousand Tongues To Sing" (words: Charles Weley, music: Carl G. Gläser)

Peter tells others about Jesus—Acts 10:1-48
   "I Love To Tell The Story" (words: Katherine Hankey, music: William G. Fischer)

Once the list is compiled, make arrangements for various people to read the scripture passages and for an instrumentalist to accompany the singing. Explain to the group that the story of Peter's life will be shared through scripture and song. Someone will read Bible verses related to part of Peter's life. Invite the group to listen to the words and to respond by singing a song associated with the theme. For variety, soloists may also share the musical messages.

Naturalist Intelligence

Learn

By arranging a display of rocks, participants will mark significant occasions in the life of Peter.

Locate

Beach stones, flat rocks, or smooth pebbles; Bible(s); Permanent markers with calligraphy tips or fine tips; Picture atlas and other reference materials; Plants (artificial or real, optional); Shallow, flat basket, dish, or tray.

Lead

Several of the disciples were known by new names when they became followers of Jesus. Peter was named Simon Bar-Jona or Simon, son of John, by his family. After Simon declared to the disciples that their leader was the Messiah (Matthew 16:16), Jesus referred to this special disciple by the Aramaic surname of *Kepha*, which means rock. Using Greek letters to transliterate the word, it comes out *Cephas*. Translated into Greek the word is *Petros*. The Greek counterpart becomes Peter in English. Matthew 16:18 records Jesus' conferring of the descriptive title: "And I tell you that you are Peter, and on this rock I will build my church, and the gates of Hades will not overcome it." (NIV) Jesus declared that Peter's confession would be the solid foundation, or the rock, of the future church. Peter was a constant companion of Jesus and many of the highlights of his life as an apostle involve rocks or stones.

Distribute Bibles and direct the group to look up the following passages and to learn about Peter:

Matthew 14:28-33—Peter attempts to walk on the water
Matthew 16:13-19—Peter's name, character, confession
Matthew 17:1-8—Peter witnesses the Transfiguration
John 20:1-10—Peter at the tomb after the Resurrection
John 21:10-17—Peter meets the resurrected Jesus
Luke 24:50-53—Peter observes Jesus' ascension.

After reading the passages, look through Bible atlases and other reference books to understand the geography of the area. It was a very rocky region. Scenes of landscape, seashore, and building consist of rocks, pebbles, or boulders. Envision Peter at the seashore. There were probably rocks in the water when he began to sink after attempting to walk toward Jesus. When Jesus and the disciples cooked breakfast on the beach, the fire pit was most likely formed with rocks. Peter was among the first witnesses to see the empty tomb after Jesus' resurrection. Following his crucifixion, Jesus was buried in a cave, which was sealed with a large boulder. Imagine the questions Peter had when he saw the heavy rock rolled away.

The scripture reports that Peter was present at two more important events in the life of Jesus: the Transfiguration and the Ascension. The Transfiguration took place on a mountain, which was a rocky site. In Luke, it is reported that Jesus led the followers to Bethany, then ascended into heaven. Pictures of surroundings will show stone buildings and rocky landscapes.

As a group or an individual project, arrange a simple display of rocks as reminders of the high points of Peter's life as someone especially chosen by Jesus. Read carefully the scripture passages and try to capture the scenes. Use a permanent marker to print or a calligraphy pen to letter the chapter and verse references. Print a few key words or draw a picture to indicate the main elements of the passage.

Place the stones in a shallow basket, dish, or tray. The stones may serve as story or prayer prompters or as a sequencing activity. Add a small plant or tiny bouquet of flowers for color and use the arrangement in a personal or classroom worship center.

Verbal/Linguistic Intelligence

Learn

By experiencing a first-person narrative, participants will comprehend biographical information regarding Saint Peter and connect the events of his life to a related Bible story, Matthew 14:22-33, and to the importance of trusting Jesus.

Locate

Bible; Basket; Costume for Fishmonger's Wife Storyteller; Fish "props" (artificial or real); Story script; Fish stickers.

Lead

Share the story of Saint Peter and tell the related Bible story as a first-person narrative. To enhance learning and to make the story memorable, a costumed "fishmonger's wife" should relate memories about her favorite saint, Peter.

"Fishmonger's Wife" Story Script
(adapted from Matthew 14:22-33)

Greetings Pilgrims! My name is Maria, the fishmonger's wife. Perhaps you know my husband, Antonio. He just came in with today's catch, and now I am on my way to sell them at the Street Fair. I know, you think fish smell bad. Many people look down upon Antonio and me because we smell like fish. It used to make me feel bad. But you know what I discovered? The first followers of Jesus—guess what they did for a living? They fished! And Peter, the one for whom our great cathedral is named, he smelled like fish when Jesus first met him. Peter is my favorite saint. From him I have learned to accept who I am and follow Jesus.

You know, Peter wasn't perfect. He sometimes made mistakes, but he always learned from them. And Jesus always helped him find strength within. In fact, Jesus changed his name from Simon to Peter, the Rock. And in Rome, we have the great church, Saint Peter's Basilica, built on the rock of Peter's faith.

I am reminded of my favorite Bible story about Saint Peter. Once when Peter was in a boat, and it was very windy, he looked out and thought he saw a ghost! But what he actually saw was Jesus walking on the water. Peter said, "Lord, if it is really you, tell me to walk on the water, too." So Jesus called him out of the boat, and Peter stepped out in faith. But soon he took his eyes off Jesus and began to look at the waves and the wind and was scared. He began to sink! He cried, "Lord, save me!" And Jesus reached out his hand and lifted Peter up. Together they got in the boat.

That story is why Peter is my favorite saint. You see, Peter wasn't always perfectly faithful. Sometimes he forgot to keep his eyes on Jesus and began to look at his problems. Do you ever do that? I do. But just like Peter, we can say, "Lord, save me!" And he will. Peter wasn't perfect. He even smelled like fish! But Peter came to accept his imperfections, trusting God to help him grow and change. And God used Peter to build the church—not the great cathedral in Rome, but the faith of Christians everywhere. Like you and me.

Well, I could talk about Saint Peter all day, but I'd better get these fish to the market. Remember, keep your eyes on Jesus, and be the best "you" you can be!

Have the fishmonger's wife give each child a fish sticker or symbol to keep.

Visual/Spatial Intelligence

Learn

By using a paper mosaic technique, participants will become familiar with symbols attributed to Saint Peter.

Locate

Bible(s); Construction paper, 9" x 12"; Envelopes; Glue and brushes or glue sticks; Magazine pages or other colorful papers; Patterns for symbols representing Saint Peter: cross, fish, keys, rock, rooster, sheep; Pencils; Pictures of early Christian or contemporary mosaics; Rulers; Scissors; Styrofoam trays or pie pans; Toothpicks or hat pins.

Lead

Each of the twelve disciples was represented by a visual symbol that indicated how he lived or died. A traditional symbol for Peter is the upside-down cross. Records of early Christian history tell us that Peter, at his own wish, was crucified with his head downward on an inverted cross. He did not feel worthy to be executed in the same manner as Jesus.

In addition to the cross, there are scriptural references to other images associated with Peter's life:

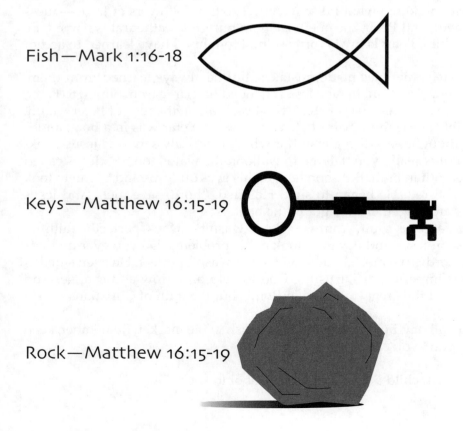

Fish—Mark 1:16-18

Keys—Matthew 16:15-19

Rock—Matthew 16:15-19

Rooster—Matthew 26:69-75

Sheep—John 21:15-19.

A number of early Christian images and symbols are represented in mosaics, an art form using small pieces of ceramic, glass, or stones anchored in mortar or plaster. The small pieces, called tesserae, fit together to form a picture. Mosaics appear in ancient buildings as decorations for ceilings, floors, and walls, as well as embellishments for courtyards and exterior walls. Look at pictures of early or modern mosaics to gain more information.

Explain that each person will assemble a paper mosaic to depict Peter's upside-down cross; then add simple cutouts of other symbols associated with his life to the background to complete the picture. Demonstrate the process for the project. Begin the paper mosaic process by first tracing or drawing the inverted cross onto a piece of light colored construction paper, nine inches square. With a pencil and a ruler, mark sections 1/2" x 12" on a sheet of construction paper in a contrasting color. Cut the long strips, then snip one-half inch squares as needed. Artists may share colors with each other. Cut textured and foil papers ahead of time and place in shallow trays for easy access.

Brush glue over a small area of the cross, then place paper bits close together on the glued surface. A toothpick or hat pin will make it easier to move paper squares into position. Continue until the cross shape is filled in with mosaic pieces. Choose one-half inch squares of a third color and follow the same procedure to fill in the background. Experiment with paper bits of different colors, sizes, and textures.

Check the scripture references and choose some or all of the other symbols to add to the mosaic background. The additional symbols can be drawn and cut out, then glued in the areas surrounding the upside-down cross.

As an option, finish the design by framing it with a border of pieces fit carefully around the edge of the background paper or with long strips of paper. Add Biblical references and titles to help observers identify the symbols.

Distribute materials for the mosaics and guide the group as they complete the activity.

Display the finished artwork so others can learn about the many facets of Peter's life. Arrange the collection of mosaic symbols as a border design along a wall or as a bulletin board display.

JULY
SAINT JAMES THE GREATER

Biography

James is a very common New Testament name derived from the Hebrew word Jacob. Because James is the name of several persons in the Bible—including another one of the disciples—it is important to distinguish the disciple known as James the Greater, from among the others. This James was the brother of John, one of the sons of Zebedee. He is usually mentioned first in relation to John, probably indicating that James was older. The two brothers were in their boat mending nets when Jesus called them to follow him (Mark 1:19-10). Later, another James, known as the son of Alphaeus, joined the group. He was known as "James the Lesser" while the son of Zebedee was given the title "James the Greater." The descriptive terms "greater" and "lesser" probably suggest age or size, not necessarily importance.

There is some speculation among scholars that Salome was James' mother, a woman who was devoted to Jesus and who witnessed the crucifixion (Matthew 27:56). Regardless of family connections, however, it is clear from scripture that James—along with his brother John and another disciple, Simon Peter—was a member of Jesus' inner circle of close friends and was someone who loved and followed Jesus. The gospels of Matthew and Mark place him at the transfiguration of Jesus (Matthew 17:1-9; Mark 9:2-8), and Matthew specifically records him with Jesus praying in the Garden of Gethsemane (Matthew 26:36-46).

While little is actually recorded about James the Greater, some factual information can be determined from the gospels as well as the Acts of the Apostles. First, the nicknames he and John were given by Jesus were "Sons of Thunder." Whether this meant that James and his brother had powerful voices, fiery tempers, or zealous commitment isn't clear. According to Mark 10:35, they did ask Jesus to be seated at his right hand in glory, which would have taken a thundering sense of importance. Apparently, James did have strong leadership skills, for after Pentecost, he became the leader of the Jerusalem Church. Ultimately, James, like the other apostles, was himself a martyr for the faith, although he is the only one whose death is mentioned in the scriptures (Acts 12:1-2). This brief sentence in Acts 12 is the only time that James is referenced individually and without his brother John.

Many stories have been handed down about this important disciple. During the years of his Christian ministry, tradition says that James traveled to Spain to spread the Gospel. After he returned to the Holy Land, he was martyred. The legend reports that his body was brought back by his disciples and buried in Spain, and thus, today James is also known as the Patron Saint of Spain.

Saint James the Greater's feast day is observed on July 25.

Mission

Not as much historical information exists about James as about disciples like Peter or even James' brother, John. We do know that James was the first apostle to give his life for the furthering of the gospel—which was probably not what he had in mind when he asked Jesus to be given a position of authority in the Kingdom. But the brash disciple learned from the death and resurrection of Jesus that to be a leader was to give oneself in service and in love, and if necessary, even to give one's life. Traditions celebrate James' missionary journey to Spain and the scallop shell is his symbol, signifying the importance of baptism and renewal.

Legacy

James represents God's re-creative power, as he is transformed from the self-serving disciple jockeying for the best place in the Kingdom, to the self-sacrificing leader of the church in Jerusalem willing to lay down his life for the Gospel. James walked closely with Jesus experiencing the majesty of Christ's transfiguration, even hearing the voice of God. From the mountaintop to the Garden of Gethsemane and along all the dusty roads in between, James observed God's power up close.

Bodily/Kinesthetic Intelligence

Learn
By actively participating in retelling the Transfiguration story, Luke 9:28-36, learners will understand the role of Saint James the Greater as one of Jesus' most trusted disciples.

Locate
"The Transfiguration" Echo Story Script.

Lead
In the story of the Transfiguration, Saint James is featured as one of three disciples Jesus invites to go with him to the mountaintop. Here the disciples see Jesus revealed in stunning light as God's chosen Messiah. They learn that their responsibility as disciples is to listen to what Jesus tells them and to follow their Master back to the valley where people are in need. Highlight from the story the role that Saint James played as one of Jesus' three closest friends.

Invite everyone to review the Biblical account of the Transfiguration by listening to and repeating phrases as the story is retold. Explain that in an "Echo Story," the leader says a line and places special emphasis on the last phrase of each sentence, the capitalized words in the script. A gesture, such as raising a palm at the point where repetition is to begin, helps give a clue to the participants to listen carefully for the words that they are to repeat. Then the leader and the participants echo or repeat these words together.

The "Transfiguration" Echo Story
(adapted from Luke 9:28-36)

Jesus took Peter and James and John UP ON THE MOUNTAINSIDE
(UP ON THE MOUNTAINSIDE)

As he was praying, Jesus was changed BEFORE THEIR VERY EYES
(BEFORE THEIR VERY EYES)

His clothing glowed brighter than any light HIS DISCIPLES HAD EVER SEEN
(HIS DISCIPLES HAD EVER SEEN)

James and the others were quite amazed BY WHAT WAS HAPPENING
(BY WHAT WAS HAPPENING)

A cloud appeared and they heard a voice THAT SEEMED TO COME FROM WITHIN
(THAT SEEMED TO COME FROM WITHIN)

The Creator of all the Universe said "THIS IS MY SON, LISTEN TO HIM!"
("THIS IS MY SON, LISTEN TO HIM!")

Jesus and Peter and James and John WERE ALL CHANGED ON THAT MOUNTAINSIDE
(WERE ALL CHANGED ON THAT MOUNTAINSIDE)

Jesus found strength for his mission and HIS FRIENDS LEARNED TO LET GOD GUIDE
(HIS FRIENDS LEARNED TO LET GOD GUIDE)

If we seek to know the Creator BY LISTENING TO JESUS, THE SON
(BY LISTENING TO JESUS, THE SON)

We will be changed by God's power TO DISCOVER WHAT WE CAN BECOME.
(TO DISCOVER WHAT WE CAN BECOME)

Interpersonal Intelligence

Learn

By playing a game of "Telephone" and sharing a snack, participants will experience the challenge to Jesus' disciples, Saint James and us, of communicating God's love with one another.

Locate

Bread; Cheese; Cups; Grapes; Napkins; Olives; Paper; Pens; Pitcher; Water.

Advance Preparation

Print the phrase "Saint James shared the message of God's love with all people near and far" on a piece of paper.

Lead

Saint James spent his days on earth sharing the message of God's love. Remind the participants that, today, we are the ones who must hear this message and pass it on. Explain that in order to remember this lesson they are going to play a game of "Telephone."

Have the learners sit in a circle or stand in a line. Give one person a written statement containing the words, "Saint James shared the message of God's love with all people near and far." Instruct this first person not to let anyone else see the message. Instead, he or she should whisper the sentence to the next person, who, in turn, whispers to the next, and so on, until the last person receives the phrase. Share the results. Point out any changes that occurred. Say that life brings changes to everyone, but stress that God works within us to help us make changes for the better. This is the message that Saint James shared in his life and in his ministry.

Celebrate by sharing a snack that disciples like Saint James might have carried with them as they took God's message to the world. Discuss that as Saint James journeyed throughout Spain, he might have brought along food like bread, cheese, grapes, and olives. Distribute these items, as well as napkins, and invite the participants to share these foods with one another. Provide water to drink, and offer a prayer together to bless God's gifts.

Intrapersonal Intelligence

Learn

By learning special titles associated with Saint James and inventing descriptive phrases for themselves, participants will further their understanding of Saint James' character and their own.

Locate

Bibles; Book of names; Paper; Pencils; Weather page from newspaper.

Lead

James the Greater was known by many names, nicknames, and titles. Some of them were "The Son of Zebedee," "The Son of Thunder," "The Leader of the Jerusalem Church," "Martyr," and "Patron Saint of Spain."

Explain to the participants that just as James had many names and titles that give us information about his character, each person's name has special meaning as well. Help the children discover or review the significance of their own names and then participate in an activity to select a descriptive nickname or phrase for themselves. Distribute paper and pencils or pens. Direct the group to fold the paper into fourths. Have each person print his or her name in the upper left-hand square. In the upper right-hand corner, tell them to write the meaning of the name and a few sentences explaining why it was selected. Use the baby book with name origins to look up the meaning of names for those who do not know or who cannot remember. In the third part of the folded paper, ask the participants to print a nickname and to add information about how it was given.

Jesus helps us understand what James was like by using the word "thunder" in his nickname. Ask the participants to think of weather or nature terms that might help people know a little more about them. Suggest phrases like "daughter of sunshine" or "son of clouds." Refer to the weather page of a newspaper for ideas, if necessary. Challenge the children to think of all types of weather or nature words and to pick one to describe themselves. In the last section of the sheet, have each person write the weather word and a few lines about why it was chosen.

Just like we can learn more about Saint James the Greater from his many names, we can discover more about classmates by sharing this information with each other. Post the finished sheets on a bulletin board and allow time for everyone to review information about the names of their classmates.

Logical/Mathematical Intelligence

Learn

By following directions to construct a Bible verse viewer, participants will create a way to continue their learning from scripture about Saint James and his relationship with Jesus.

Locate

Bibles; Brass paper fasteners; Circle patterns, 8" and 12" diameter (paper plates or pizza boards); Heavy paper; Markers, fine-tipped; Pencils; Rulers; Scissors; Tape.

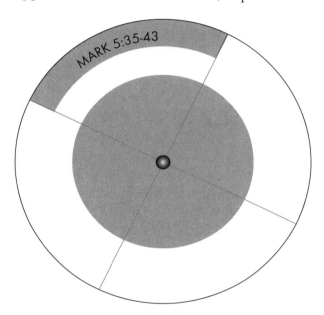

Lead

James the Greater, was one of the disciples in the inner circle of Jesus' closest friends along with Peter and John. James the Greater, must have been very close to Jesus because he witnessed several significant events, including the raising of Jairus' daughter, the Transfiguration of Jesus on the mountain, the healing of Peter's mother-in-law, and the agony of Jesus in the Garden of Gethsemane.

Construct a Bible verse viewer to illustrate some important occasions that included James the Greater with Jesus. Using the larger circle pattern, copy and cut two circles from the heavy paper. Next, trace and cut out the small circle. Mark lines dividing each circle into fourths. In each of the sections of the small circle, draw a picture illustrating the scenes witnessed by James. Use the Bible to discover what happened in the following passages:

Jesus' raising of Jairus' daughter: Mark 5:35-43

Jesus' Transfiguration: Matthew 17:1-9; Mark 9:2-8

Jesus' praying at Gethsemane: Matthew 26:36-46

Jesus' healing Peter's mother-in-law: Mark 1:29-31.

Take one of the large circles for the inside layer of the Bible verse viewer. Cut a two-inch slit into one quarter of the circle and continue around the outside to cut away a curved strip in that quarter. This forms a viewing window.

On the outside edge of the remaining circle, write the four scripture passages, spacing them five or six inches apart. Be sure the writing fits within the open area of the viewing window.

Assemble the viewer by stacking the circles in this order: 1) on the bottom, place the piece with the written verses, 2) next put the "window" piece and 3) on top, position the small circle displaying the pictures. Carefully punch a brass paper fastener into the center of the stacked circles and secure the fastener behind the bottom piece. Turn the bottom circle to display writing, then rotate the small circle until the picture and the verse match.

Distribute materials to the participants and supervise the construction process. After the viewers are created, encourage each person to share the teaching tool with someone who does not know about Saint James the Greater.

Musical/Rhythmic Intelligence

Learn

By making rhythm instruments, participants will associate the culture of Spain with its patron Saint, James the Greater.

Locate

Cassette or CD player; Duct tape; Hammer; Blocks of wood; Lids (plastic with rounded edges) from frozen juice cans; Nails; Pencils; Castanets (Optional); Recordings of Spanish music; Sandpaper.

Lead

People of Spain, the country of which James the Greater is the patron saint, appreciate rhythmic folk songs and colorful dances, such as the bolero, fandango, and flamenco. Musical accompaniment usually include guitars and rhythm instruments. Spanish dancers use castanets to click out the tempo of the music. Traditional instruments are made of hard wood and are shaped like small cymbals. They are used in pairs, held in one hand and are clicked together to create the distinctive sound.

Every culture has rhythm instruments made from materials at hand—gourds, shells, sticks, stones, and other supplies. Make "castanets" from plentiful and recyclable resources.

Demonstrate the process for making castanets. Select a block of wood and sand away any rough spots to avoid splinters. Select two or three clean juice lids, dot the centers with a permanent marker; then use a hammer and a long nail to pound a hole through each lid.

Stack the lids so that the holes line up; then push the nail through the holes. Hammer the nail about one-half inch into the wood base. When the nail is pounded securely into the wood, shake the instrument to see if the lids move back and forth making a clattering sound. If the lids do not slide easily, remove the nail and replace it with a thinner one. Cover a portion of the wood block with duct tape to get a better grip when playing the "castanets."

Distribute supplies for the project and guide the group as they construct castanets.

Listen to recordings of Spanish folk music or dance tunes and click out the tempo with the new rhythm instruments. Write phrases about the life of Saint James and recite them to the rhythm. One example is:

Saint James the Greater
The Son of Thunder
Followed his Master
Became a church leader.

Naturalist Intelligence

Learn

By decorating a picture frame with shells, participants will connect the symbol with the life of Saint James.

Locate

Cardboard or mats (the kind used inside picture frames); Construction paper; Mat knives; Pencils; Photograph of each participant; Rulers; Scissors; Shells, assorted sizes; Tacky glue or glue gun and glue sticks; Tape.

Lead

Legends tell us that Saint James the Greater was the first missionary to preach the gospel in Spain. Tradition holds that after James was killed in Jerusalem, his body was buried in Spain where the Cathedral of Santiago de Compostela now stands.

We do know for certain that the Apostle James is the patron saint of Spain. During the Middle Ages, the Cathedral of Santiago de Compostela was an important site for pilgrimages. Because the scallop shell was the symbol for James the Greater, shells became the badges of pilgrims who traveled to this site. The familiar symbol for James includes three scallop shells, which represent his missionary journeys. Sometimes, James is symbolized by a single scallop shell and a sword, which depicts the way he died.

Explain that each participant will decorate a picture frame with shells, then use it to display a photograph. This will be a reminder that each person, as well as James, can be a missionary by sharing Jesus' teachings.

Demonstrate the process for the project. Select a piece of cardboard or a mat to fit the photograph. To form a mat, mark the cardboard and carefully cut an opening a little smaller than the photo. Use caution when cutting with a mat knife and protect the table with an extra piece of cardboard. Select enough shells to cover the mat. Glue the shells in place. When the glue is dry, tape a photo to the back of the frame. Cut a piece of construction paper to fit the back of the frame. Glue the paper in place to protect the photo.

Distribute supplies for the activity and guide the group as they construct shell-covered picture frames. Challenge each participant to give the framed photograph to someone special and to share the story of Saint James with that person.

Verbal/Linguistic Intelligence

Learn

By experiencing a first-person narrative, participants will comprehend biographical information regarding Saint James and connect the events of his life to a related Bible story, Luke 9:28-36, and to the importance of listening to Jesus.

Locate

Bible; Costume for "innkeeper" storyteller; Shells or shell stickers; Story script .

Lead

Share the story of James the Greater and tell the related Bible story as a first-person narrative. To enhance learning and to make the story memorable, a costumed "innkeeper" should relate memories about her favorite saint, James.

"Innkeeper" Story Script
(adapted from Luke 9:28-36)

Greetings! My name is Angela; I am the keeper of an inn along *el Camino de Santiago*—that means "the road of Saint James." Thousands of people pass my way on their pilgrimage to and from the great cathedral. God has given me the privilege of taking care of these travelers as they journey. I cannot think of a better way to earn a living! I get to live in the beautiful countryside surrounded by green fields and herds of peaceful sheep. Near me is a forest, edged by wild blackberries and trees topped with glossy holly. All around me are reminders of God our Creator. But most important of all are the people, the pilgrims on their way to visit the silver statue of Saint James at the Cathedral.

Saint James is the patron saint of Spain, you know. There are those who try to tell us that our beloved Santiago never visited here; but we believe that, after Herod ordered James killed for his faith in Jesus, James' body was brought back and his bones buried here where he had been a missionary. He shared the message that God's love in Christ can change each of us.

Saint James knew what it meant to change! He was nicknamed "Son of Thunder" by Jesus because of his quick temper. Once James got in trouble with the other disciples because he demanded to be the most important man in God's kingdom. Jesus knew that James still had a lot to learn about being a disciple. Maybe that is why Jesus chose James to go up the mountain that day.

Have you heard the story of the Transfiguration? Do you know what happened? No? Well, Jesus took Peter, James, and John and climbed the highest mountain. At the top while the disciples were resting, exhausted from the climb, Jesus was praying. Moses and Elijah appeared to Jesus, and Jesus' clothing seemed to shine like the very sun itself. Well, the light woke up the disciples, and they were dumbfounded by what they saw. Peter started babbling something about building a special place to worship there on the mountain, when suddenly all three of them were surrounded by a cloud. Can you imagine what that would look like? They weren't even able to see Jesus and his bright light anymore. From the cloud came a voice: "This is my beloved Son; listen to him." They had heard the voice of God.

Then, just as suddenly, the cloud disappeared, and they could see Jesus once more, only he just looked ordinary. Jesus told them not to tell anyone about the experience, and they didn't until after Jesus rose from the dead. I think when you've seen a transformation like that, you can never be the same again.

That is why I love keeping the inn on the *el Camino de Santiago*. I have seen so many people changed by their pilgrimage to the holy cathedral. I have helped those so sick that I thought they could never finish the last miles of their journey. And then, when they are returning, I see them renewed, healthy, enthusiastic about living for God.

When I have held a cool drink to parched lips, the receiver often tells me I am an angel. That is somewhat true for my name, Angela, means "angel." But angels are messengers. And when the pilgrims share their stories of God's blessing with me, it is they who become God's messengers for me. Sometimes they bring me a shell from the shore where they were baptized. You know a shell is the symbol for pilgrims who travel to *Santiago de Compostela* because it is the emblem of Saint James.

Saint James brought us our message from God. He taught us Christ's love. Love that could transform a selfish, outspoken man into a committed disciple who would give his life for his faith. My prayer is that like our Saint James, you may find Christ's life-changing love, too.

Have the innkeeper give each child a shell or a shell sticker to keep after telling the story.

Visual/Spatial Intelligence

Learn

By adding their own footprints to display on a banner, participants will follow the pattern of Saint James to affirm their commitment to follow Jesus in all of life.

Locate

Chalk; Chalkboard erasers; Fine point markers; Large roll of paper, e.g., brown craft or dark-colored bulletin board paper; Paint brushes; Pattern for footprints; Reference books on Spain and the Cathedral of Saint James; Rubber cement; Rulers and yardsticks; Scissors; Sponges, small; Spools or small wood blocks; Tempera paints, assorted colors.

Advance Preparation

Cut rolled paper to about 3' x 5'. Fold under the ends cut from the roll. Pre-draw outlines of the scenes especially if working with young children. Make footprint stamps by cutting two or three sizes of right and left feet from small sponges. Glue each "foot" sponge to a spool or wood block. Cover sponges with different colors of tempera paint.

Lead

Santiago de Compostela, the site of the Shrine of Saint James the Greater, is in the northwestern part of Spain. Some pilgrims traveled by sea and others trekked through the hilly and mountainous terrain to reach this revered destination in the region of Galicia. The name Compostela comes from the Latin *Campus Stellae* which means "Field of the Star." It is reported that in the seventh century, a star shone over a field where the tomb of the apostle James was discovered. Saint James of the Starry Field, *Santiago de Compostela*, became the patron saint of Spain. Other writers believe the name "Compostela" is a variation of the Spanish term "Giacomo Postolo," James the Apostle.

There have been many additions and changes to the ornate Basilica built in honor of the Saint James. The main part of the church and its original portico were completed in the 1100's; the current facade which covers the first entrance, dates to the eighteenth century. Think of the millions of feet that have walked the rocky routes to this shrine. Encourage the students to join with fellow pilgrims to paint a mural banner depicting this special site.

Use brown craft paper or dark colored bulletin board paper for the background. Set the paper either vertically or horizontally. Lightly sketch jagged mountains across the paper, near the top. Copy and enlarge a photo of the cathedral to paste on the background or draw a simplified version of the church. As an alternative, design a large cross in front of the mountains. Ask for a few volunteers to draw the outlines and others to paint the scenes. Remember to place a large star in the sky.

Everyone can participate by adding footprints leading to the famous shrine in honor of Saint James. Invite the learners to choose a right and left foot stamp—small, medium or large. Help them press each "foot" onto a tempera paint filled sponge—one color per student; then continue to stamp the footprints on the paper. When the paint is dry, print initials on the printed feet. The colorful footprints will represent all the different travelers on this faith journey to honor Saint James. Display the banner for all to enjoy.

AUGUST
SAINT CLARE

Biography

Clare was born into a noble family near Assisi, Italy in either 1193 or 1194. Her father, Favarone, was a count, and her mother, Ortulana, was known as a virtuous woman. Clare had two sisters named Agnes and Beatrice.

From her youth, Clare was devout, living a life of prayer and service. She refused proposals for marriage, preferring to dedicate her life to spiritual pursuits. When she was eighteen, Saint Francis came to preach the Lenten sermons at a church in Assisi. Clare was inspired by Francis' words. Privately she sought him out, asking if she might live as he taught, following Christ completely. On Palm Sunday in 1212, Clare went to Mass at the cathedral. Although she did not go to the altar as the other noblewomen did to receive the palms, the bishop came to her and placed a palm in her hand. Later, many saw this as a sign of the church's blessing on what Clare was about to do.

In the middle of the night on Palm Sunday, Clare secretly left her parent's home and made her way to Francis and his Poor Friars at the small chapel of the Portiuncula. Francis and the brothers received her, and she put aside her wealthy clothing to put on the rough tunic and thick veil that would henceforth be her covering. Francis placed Clare in the care of the Benedictine sisters. When her family discovered she was gone, they came to physically remove her, but withdrew because the Benedictine sanctuary prohibited force of any kind. Later, also against the wishes of their family, Agnes joined her sister. Together they formed the Order of Poor Ladies, or Poor Clares, the Second Order of Saint Francis. Eventually her widowed mother and her second sister joined them as well.

In the eyes of God, Clare believed that all persons were equal. She saw herself as the servant of those who worked with her. In the monastery, Clare took on the most menial tasks. Together she and the other sisters worked with their hands and begged alms for their own support. Their lives were devoted to prayer, hard work, and good deeds. At age twenty-one, Clare agreed to accept the role of Abbess, but for nearly forty years, she never used the term. She lived among the sisters as one who served.

After a long illness, Clare died in 1253, and was buried in the San Giorgio church where Saint Francis had first been interred until his body was relocated to a new basilica. Two years later, Clare was canonized as a saint, and August 11 was designated as her feast day. Clare's remains were later moved to a crypt at Santa Chiara for display.

Mission

Clare's primary mission was to lead a life of poverty, devotion, and hard work. Twice her dedication seemed to provide special protection for the city that housed her monastery. First she and the Poor Ladies prayed that the city would be spared from the ravage of the Holy Roman Emperor Frederick II; then Clare offered herself as a hostage if the army would leave. They departed without doing any harm. Another time when capture threatened, Clare had all the sisters anoint themselves with ashes and report to the chapel to pray. The soldiers left the next morning.

Clare and the Poor Ladies embraced charity, humility, and poverty as companions for their spiritual journey. While the gospels formed their central focus, the example and inspiration of Francis also provided a key influence on their work.

Legacy

Although she rarely left the monastery, living a disciplined life of prayer and service, Clare's ministry had a lasting impact on others. While her devotion and hard work made a difference in the time period in which she lived—for her kindness and good works were legendary—the results of Clare's efforts are most felt today through the Order she fought to establish and protect. After the death of Saint Francis in 1226, her religious rule was threatened because the Franciscan brothers were not allowed to serve as preachers to the Poor Clares any longer. Clare argued that if the brothers were not allowed to serve them spiritually, then they would also no longer accept the food the brothers provided for them physically. Clare's "hunger strike" brought the desired results; her Order was sanctioned, and the Franciscan brothers and priests became permanently attached to the Poor Clares.

Today, the Order of the Poor Clares still exists. They continue to follow the teachings of Saint Francis, radiating the joy and peace that comes from living in Christian poverty.

Bodily/Kinesthetic Intelligence

Learn

By constructing paper tube puppets and using them to explore the needs of others, participants will understand Saint Clare's "Privilege of Poverty."

Locate

Bible; Craft sticks or dowel rods; Fabric scraps; Fake fur, Fiberfil or yarn; Felt; Glue; Paper tubes, two contrasting sizes; Scissors.

Advance Preparation

Locate information on organizations that serve the poor such as:

Fellowship of the Least Coin
Church Women United
475 Riverside Drive, Suite 500
New York, New York 10115
212-870-2347

Heifer International
P. O. Box 8058
Little Rock, AR 72203
800-422-0474

UNICEF
Three UN Plaza
New York, NY 10017
212-326-7000

Lead

Through the virtue of poverty, Clare identified with Christ who "made himself poor for our sake" (2 Corinthians 8:9). Saint Clare considered poverty a privilege. For Clare, poverty meant being more concerned with the things of God than with the things of the world. For example, when Clare received a large inheritance after the death of her father, she gave the whole amount to the poor without reserving any of it for the needs of her Order. In 1216, Clare officially obtained the "Privilege of Poverty" from Pope Innocent III, which granted permission for her nuns to live totally on alms, without possessing any personal or communal property. From time to time, Saint Clare had to fight to maintain this privilege against the modifications desired by church authorities. When Cardinal Hugolino became Pope Gregory IX, Clare asked him to reconfirm the "Privilege of Poverty." A Church document given on September 17, 1228, assured Clare of the Church's official recognition of her radical choice.

Clare's "Privilege of Poverty" still sets an example for God's people to follow. It challenges Christians to live with less anxiety about possessions and with more generosity about sharing God's blessings with others. Even the smallest gift can make a difference. Read Mark 12:41-44 to the class. The widow's offering was a mite, the smallest coin, yet her generosity was praised. A penny, combined with other pennies, can do great things. Teach the students about groups that use pennies to help the poor.

Then make "puppets for pennies" and develop skits about the people who have been helped by these organizations.

Ask the participants if they have ever heard of groups such as "Fellowship of the Least Coin," "Heifer Project," or "UNICEF." Least Coin is an organization that collects pennies from people all over the world. The gathered money is spent to build hospitals and schools in many different countries. Heifer Project uses pennies to provide live animals for hungry people. The people breed the animals and soon they have chickens, sheep, cows, or goats. The recipients then give an animal, or a pair, to another person to breed, and the cycle continues. Through the pennies that UNICEF receives from "trick-or-treat" boxes, they provide immunizations for children around the world who need health care.

Organize the participants into three groups to create puppet plays. If the class is small, choose fewer options; if it is large, have more than one group develop other similar plays. The skits will highlight people who have been helped by the pennies given by others. Use the following themes for the skits:

- a family that received a calf from Heifer Project;
- children who were given life-saving immunizations by UNICEF;
- students attending a school built by Least Coin.

Instruct the group members to plan their skits. Each should choose a country where the story takes place, as well as the actions they will portray. When characters have been chosen, the learners can create puppets to play the various parts. Demonstrate the process for turning paper tubes, of any size, into puppets. Use a small tube, such as a toilet paper roll, a medium tube, like a paper towel core, or a large tube, such as a wrapping paper roll.

Form the puppet face by cutting a piece of felt and gluing it to the top one-third of the tube. Make facial features from felt scraps and glue them in place. Attach fake fur, Fiberfil, or yarn to the top of the tube for hair. Glue a piece of felt around the remainder of the tube to serve as the undergarment. Layers of fabric in contrasting or complementary colors can be added as over garments. Make arms from strips of cloth or felt and glue them to the sides of the tube. Apply a craft stick to the inside back of the tube to serve as the rod by which the puppet is operated.

Provide supplies for the project and guide the students as they complete the puppet-making process. When everyone is finished, allow time for each group to use their puppets to practice their skits. When all groups are ready, present the plays. Conclude by encouraging the students to live their lives in the spirit of Saint Clare. Challenge them to be less concerned about possessions and more purposeful in sharing God's gifts with others.

Interpersonal Intelligence

Learn

By tracing their own roots of personal faith in Jesus, participants will see how God's plan works best when they, like Clare, are mentored by God's people.

Locate

Coffee cans; Construction paper, felt, or poster board; Fabric or foil; Glue; Hole punch; Paper clips; Pencils or pens; Ribbon, string, or yarn; Scissors; Stones; Tree branches.

Lead

Clare of Assisi was inspired by the example of Saint Francis to make her commitment to the religious life. Francis was a mentor—a spiritual guide—to Clare, helping her focus her life of faith on the teachings of the gospels. Both Francis and Clare sought to imitate Christ and their vows of poverty freed them to live simply in the footsteps of Jesus. Francis helped Clare discover the principles of the monastic life and guided her as she established her own religious community, the Poor Clares. Then Clare became a mentor to many other women who entered the Order Francis helped her to form. Every Christian has many mentors, people who serve as influences on their faith development. As an individual or a group project, prepare a "Faith Tree"—based on the model of the "Jesse Tree"—to help the participants trace the roots of their personal faith in Jesus and to name some of the people who have influenced their religious formation.

Explain that a Jesse Tree is frequently used during the season of Advent, the four-week period proceeding Christmas. It incorporates symbols that recall important people and events that are a significant part of Jesus' ancestry. A Jesse Tree is much like a family tree. It is named for the Father of David, who lived about one thousand years before Jesus. The prophecy predicting the coming of the "branch of Jesse" is found in Isaiah 11.

Traditionally, symbols on a Jesse Tree correspond to stories recorded in Old and New Testament scripture passages. Each event or person, such as Adam and Eve, Noah, Ruth, Isaiah, and John the Baptist, prepared the world for Jesus in a unique way. During a season such as Advent, or any time throughout the year, help the participants trace the roots of their belief in Jesus by using this activity.

Begin by inviting each person to prepare a base for the Faith Tree. Cover a large coffee can with a piece of fabric or foil. Tie ribbon around the top of the material to hold it in place. Set the tree branch in the center of the can and fill the container with stones to anchor the limb. This will serve as the base to hold the symbols that trace the roots of faith in Jesus.

Cut shapes such as circles, squares, and triangles, out of construction paper, felt, or poster board. Invite each person to choose enough shapes to correspond with the length of time of the project—seven for a week, thirty for a month, and so forth. Instruct class members to print the name of a significant person from their faith journey on each piece. Suggest people such as: mother, father, grandmother, grandfather, sister, brother, husband, wife, son, daughter, pastor, teacher, catechist, youth group leader, neighbor, co-worker, camp counselor, choir director, Christian Education director, mid-week program coordinator, friend, religion teacher, and even stranger. Add details with marker drawings, photos, illustrations, or decorative trims.

Poke a hole at the top of each symbol and attach an opened paper clip to serve as an ornament hanger. Then invite each learner to choose a different personal symbol each day—in chronological order, if possible—and connect it to the branch. Complete the activity by looking up Bible passages on faith, including the chapter on the faith of our Christian ancestors in Hebrews 11. Display the unique "trees" as reminders of ways in which our personal connection to Jesus has been influenced by God's people.

Intrapersonal Intelligence

Learn

By experiencing a form of prayer called *Lectio Divina*, participants will understand the importance of contemplation in the life of Saint Clare and discover their own need to be open to God's Spirit.

Locate

Bibles.

Lead

Clare, as well as her Poor Clares, knew the importance and power of prayer. Life in the monastery centered around seeking the Holy Spirit's presence, from Matins, or morning prayers, to Compline, or last prayers of the day. In both private and public prayer, the Poor Clares sought the will of God. Saint Clare even woke the sisters at midnight to remind them to praise God. Others wrote about Clare's tears in prayer and her long periods of contemplation. Clare prayed day and night; she prayed in times of difficulty and in times of rejoicing; she prayed for her sisters and her friends as well as for the needs of the entire world.

Clare set an example for us to devote more of our lives to prayer and contemplation. Today there is a renewed emphasis on an ancient form of prayer called *Lectio Divina*, praying with scriptures. Experience the practice of *Lectio Divina*. In this form of prayer, each participant waits for the Holy Spirit to speak through scripture as a source of inspiration and reflection. The emphasis is on listening and quiet contemplation. In today's rushed existence, *Lectio Divina* offers a method for quieting the soul and for opening the mind to God's Word.

Locate Romans 8:26-27 in a bible and read the verses to the class. Then tell the group that they will use an ancient method of reflecting on God's Word, called *Lectio Divina*, to meditate on this passage. Instruct each learner to find a partner, or form small groups of three to four persons. Be sure that each participant has a bible. Begin by explaining the process for *Lectio Divina*, a contemplative praying of the scriptures as listed below:

1. One person reads aloud the scripture passage, then repeats the passage again. Others are attentive to a segment they find especially meaningful to them.

2. Everyone keeps silence for one to two minutes while each person silently repeats a word or phrase that is important.

3. Each person takes a turn to share aloud the word or phrase that was attractive to him or her.

4. Another person reads the passage again aloud.

5. Everyone keeps silence for two to three minutes. Ask the students to reflect based on the question "Where does the content of this reading touch my life today?"

6. Share aloud using phrases that begin with "I hear . . ." and "I see . . ."

7. A third person reads the passage out loud.

8. Everyone keeps silence for one to two minutes. Ask the participants to reflect on the phrase "I believe that God wants me to . . . ."

9. Call on the participants to share their reflections with the other(s).

10. After everyone has had an opportunity to speak, encourage the students to pray aloud or silently for their partner or the people in the group.

Once everyone is comfortable with the guidelines, follow the process and prayerfully reflect on Romans 8:26-27 and its meaning for each person's life.

Logical/Mathematical Intelligence

Learn

By participating in a form of intercession called a bidding prayer, learners will follow the example of Clare and the Poor Ladies of remembering the needs of people of the world.

Locate

Globe or world map; Music for "Jesus Loves the Little Children" (George F. Root).

Lead

Clare of Assisi's Order of Poor Ladies was built on a foundation of prayer. It was the privilege of these religious women to spend large portions of each day in both communal and private prayer. As a group, their lives were woven together through conversations with God rather than with each other. Although the Poor Clares were strictly cloistered (separated from the world), prayer for the world was their central focus. They concentrated the energy of their hearts and their minds to intercede for the needs of God's people. Clare's example, and that of her followers, inspires us to make a commitment to pray for the people of the world, too.

Invite the participants to offer a series of petitions for the needs of the world by using the pattern of a bidding prayer, also called a directed or a guided prayer. Explain that the leader suggests topics related to a situation and guides the group to offer thoughts connected to the theme. After each subject, the leader invites the participants to offer a silent prayer for the people named in the phrase.

Since "Jesus Loves the Little Children" is a familiar chorus, as well as the emphasis of Christ's message and Clare's ministry, use it as the basis of a bidding prayer. Ask the class to sing the first verse together:

> "Jesus loves the little children,
> all the children of the world.
> Red, brown, yellow, black, and white,
> they are precious in God's sight.
> Jesus loves the little children of the world."

Invite the group to participate in a prayer in which they, like Saint Clare of Assisi and her Order of the Poor Ladies, can remember children in all parts of the world. Sing the first two lines of the song again. Stop after the phrase "all the children of the world." Display the globe or world map. Explain that the seven continents will be named and that a brief pause will follow each statement. Encourage the group to pray for the people of that particular region during the silence. Suggest that they remember the physical, as well as the spiritual needs, of the people in that place.

Name each continent: Africa, Antarctica, Asia, Australia, Europe, North America, and South America, and pause briefly after each. After the prayer, sing the remainder of the song and conclude with "Amen."

Musical/Rhythmic Intelligence

Learn

By using the hymn "When I Survey the Wondrous Cross" and participating in a cross-cube activity, students will reflect on the importance of the cross of Christ in Clare's life and their own.

Locate

Cube pattern; Construction paper; Duplicating equipment; Markers; Music for "When I Survey the Wondrous Cross" (words: Isaac Watts, music: Lowell Mason); Paper; Pencils; Scissors; Tape.

Advance Preparation

Enlarge the cube pattern to the desired size and duplicate copies for the participants to share.

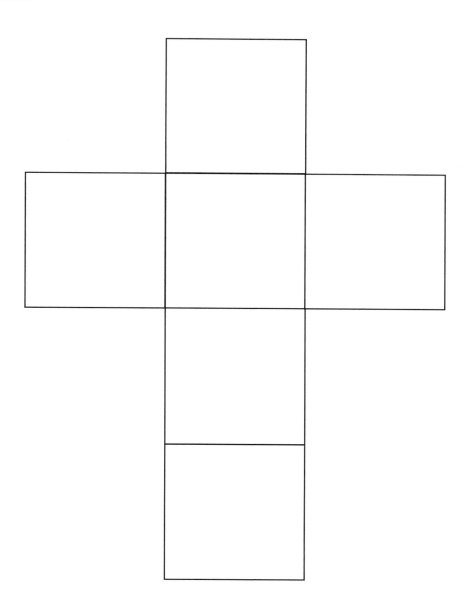

Lead

Although the famous hymn writer, Isaac Watts (1674-1748) lived nearly 500 years after Clare of Assisi (1194-1253), the words of his familiar hymn "When I Survey the Wondrous Cross" could have been the saint's personal statement of faith. Isaac Watts' words read:

When I survey the wondrous cross,
on which the Christ of glory died,
My richest gain I count but loss,
and pour contempt on all my pride.

Were the whole realm of nature mine,
that were a present far too small;
Love so amazing, so divine,
demands my soul, my life, my all.

The cross was the central symbol of Clare's faith. She once wrote a friend saying, "Take up the cross and follow Christ who has gone before us." When Clare prayed for those who were ill, Clare made the sign of the cross and murmured words for their recovery. To others, she spoke of the cross as a mirror in which we must gaze to see ourselves reflected in Christ.

One of the ways to contemplate on the meaning of the cross is through music. Locate the song "When I Survey the Wondrous Cross" in a hymnbook and sing it as a group. Or, find the music on a recording and play it for the class. Explain that the author of the words for the hymn "When I Survey the Wondrous Cross" was Isaac Watts. He grew up in England in a very religious family. Isaac was very smart, and by the time he was five, he learned to understand Latin; by age nine, he knew Greek; at eleven, he added French; and at thirteen, he knew Hebrew—all in addition to being fluent in English. Isaac began to write hymn texts as a young man, and during his lifetime, he composed about 750 hymns. Two of his most famous are the Christmas carol "Joy to the World" and the Lenten hymn, "When I Survey the Wondrous Cross."

"When I Survey the Wondrous Cross" reminds us that when we look at the cross, we see it as Christ's gift of love to us. Isaac Watts tells us that such an amazing gift requires us to give something back in response: our souls, our lives, our all. Since the cross was such an important symbol in Clare's life, create a folded paper cross-cube and use it to represent the story of the hymn, Clare's story, and the personal stories of the participants.

Distribute a piece of construction paper and a pencil to each pupil. Place cross-cube patterns and scissors within sharing distance of the students. Instruct the group to trace the pattern onto the paper and to cut out the shape. Direct the students to print "When I Survey the Wondrous Cross" in the top square of one side of the shape and "Saint Clare of Assisi" in the top square of the reverse side of the cross. Next, tell them to print the words Who, What, When, Where, and Why in the remaining five squares on each side of the paper. As a group, discuss answers to each of the five "W" questions related to the event of Christ's sacrifice on the cross. Guide the participants as they record the group's ideas on the two sides. Show the students how to fold each section toward the center to form a cube and provide tape to secure the flaps.

After completing the project, invite the students to draw another cross-cube and to complete the "Who, What, When, Where, and Why" answers from their personal experience of sacrifice for the Lord. As respondents think about how they personally accept the cross of Christ, they should remember Clare's advice to see our lives reflected in the cross of Christ. Invite the participants to think about how Christ's cross affects who we are, what we do, when we live, where we go, why we make choices, and how we share our faith. As the group completes this portion of the project, challenge them to remember the gift of love represented by the cross.

Naturalist Intelligence

Learn

By constructing palm branches, participants will re-tell the events of Clare's life that occurred on the Palm Sunday when her ministry was blessed.

Locate

Construction paper, green; Glue; Paint brushes; Paper towel tubes or cardboard rolls from hangers; Pens or markers; Scissors; Tape; Tempera paint, green.

Lead

Palm Sunday, 1212, was an important day in the life of Clare of Assisi. In the morning she attended Mass at the cathedral, but when the others went to the altar rail to receive a palm, she remained in her place in the pew. Nevertheless, the bishop went to her and placed a branch in her hands. Recollecting on this act later, many witnesses came to see it as the bishop's approval of Clare's plan to follow God's leading in her life. That same night, Clare secretly left her family home—accompanied by her Aunt Bianca and another companion. Saint Francis and his followers met the women at the small chapel of the Portiuncula. There Francis helped Clare exchange her fine clothing and her wealthy lifestyle for a rough robe and a future with "Lady Poverty." Francis and the brothers accompanied Clare to the Monastery of San Paolo in Bastia where she found sanctuary with the Benedictines. Although Clare's Uncle Monaldo came with force to reclaim her, he withdrew because the sacred property was reserved as a sanctuary from violence. Later Clare moved to San Angelo in Panzo, where she was joined by her younger sister Agnes. After the little church of San Damiano was repaired, they assumed residence in that location.

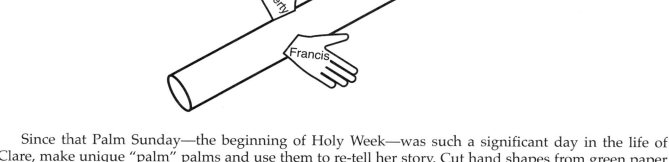

Since that Palm Sunday—the beginning of Holy Week—was such a significant day in the life of Clare, make unique "palm" palms and use them to re-tell her story. Cut hand shapes from green paper for the "palm" leaves. Write words that explain various parts of Clare's story on each shape. Be sure to include Clare, Francis, Palm Sunday, and 1212. Paint the tube or paper roll green. Set it aside to dry. Glue or tape the palms along the stem or paper roll.

Provide the supplies for the project and guide the learners as they create their own "palm" branches. Once the branches are completed, allow time to re-tell the story of the events of Saint Clare's life that occurred on this Holy Day.

Verbal/Linguistic Intelligence

Learn

By experiencing a first-person narrative, participants will comprehend biographical information regarding Saint Clare of Assisi and connect the events of her life to a related Bible story, Matthew 4:18-22, and to the importance of discipleship.

Locate

Bible; Costume for "Mother" Storyteller; Story Script.

Lead

Share the story of Saint Clare of Assisi and tell the related Bible story of Jesus calling the disciples as a first-person narrative. To enhance learning and to make the story memorable, a costumed "mother" should relate memories about her favorite saint, Clare.

"Mother" Story Script
(adapted from Matthew 4:18-22)

Peace to you, my children! My name is Ortulana. I am one of the Poor Clares from the monastery at San Damiano. I wasn't always considered a "poor" lady. In fact, I was born into a wealthy knight's family, and I married a rich and powerful count, as well. We had three daughters: Clare, Agnes, and Beatrice. Favarone and I thought that our daughters would also marry well and become great ladies. However, our daughter Clare had a different future in mind. She had always been a devout and faithful Christian. We taught her to be loving and giving. But once Clare heard Saint Francis of Assisi preach of his way of poverty and sacrifice for Christ, she became convinced that she would live the Gospel as he did.

Clare's father was furious when she slipped away during the night—on Palm Sunday—to join Francis' mission. We tried everything to get her to come home, but it was no use. She had found something more meaningful than a life of ease and prosperity. Soon our daughter Agnes left us to join her sister and the other "Poor Ladies," as they had come to be called. Once my husband died, I, too, along with Beatrice, decided to join my daughter in her efforts to follow Christ.

Clare always reminded me of the first disciples. Scripture teaches us that the fishermen heard the message of Jesus and "immediately left their nets and followed him." *Immediately*. That was the enthusiasm that Clare had for following Jesus. Her life of devotion and simplicity was patterned after the example set by Saint Francis, but both of them really sought to live in total dependence upon God as they followed Christ.

That is why we have no shoes, eat no meat, live in poverty, and spend our time in silent prayer. Do you think we want you to feel sorry for us? No! We have found what makes life truly rich. The peace and contentment we find in following Christ cannot be purchased no matter how wealthy you are. When you find something truly valuable, you are willing to give up everything you own in order to possess it. The first disciples of Christ knew that. Why else did they leave their nets and follow immediately? Clare knew the value of responding to God's call, even before her parents understood.

I am thankful that she taught me how to live life in humble simplicity. Remember that all of us must share what we learn from God, sometimes even teaching our parents. Go in peace. Let God guide your steps. Simple acts for God can change the world. Clare believed that, and now I do, too.

Visual/Spatial Intelligence

Learn

By creating squares for an altar cloth or a banner, participants will connect active involvement with the example of Clare's work for others.

Locate

Backing material (optional); Fabric; Permanent markers, paint sticks, or liquid embroidery pens; Scissors; Sewing equipment; "Wonder Under" (optional).

Advance Preparation

Cut a 4" x 4" or larger fabric square per person. Decide on the size of the squares by determining the number of participants. If many people are involved, the squares should be cut smaller. If only a few work on the project, the squares should be cut larger.

Lead

Clare believed in the power of working for others. Even when she was ill, Clare would keep her hands busy by making small cloths, called corporals, on which the bread and the wine of the Eucharist would be placed. She distributed these cloths among all of the churches in Assisi. Clare believed that a balance of work and prayer protected the soul from idleness and fostered devotion to God.

Just like Clare, we can use our time and our talents to be a blessing to others. Talk with the students to discuss ideas about the talents that God has given them and ways in which they could use these gifts to make a difference in the world. For example, a learner who has a flair for music could volunteer to sing in a choir; someone with artistic ability could decorate bookmarks with Bible verses to give to shut-ins; another whose talent is acting could perform a Bible story for another class.

Combine the thoughts and the talents of the young people, or of an entire parish, as they work together to make a patchwork altar cloth, worship center cover, or banner illustrating ways of sharing their talents to serve God. This project involves the cooperation and invites the contributions of many individuals. The finished product will serve as a reminder of what can be accomplished when people work individually and collectively to use their time and talents in God's service.

Distribute a piece of cloth to each person. Provide the supplies needed to decorate the squares. These could be permanent markers, liquid embroidery pens, or paint sticks. Encourage the participants to decorate their squares with meaningful symbols and words.

When everyone is finished, determine the arrangement of the squares. Sew the patches together by hand or by machine, or iron them onto a background using a bonding material such as "Wonder Under." If a finished back is desired, cut a plain piece of fabric the size of the completed banner to use for a backing. Place the right sides of the banner and the background together. Stitch the backing to the patchwork, leaving the bottom end open. Turn right side out. Slipstitch the bottom seam.

If the patchwork piece is to be used as a banner, stitch a casing or add loops to the top of the cloth. Insert a pole or rod for hanging the work.

Display the patchwork piece in a prominent place to remind the participants, and the parish, of their commitment to use their talents and their time to share God's love with other people.

SEPTEMBER
SAINT HILDEGARD OF BINGEN

Biography

Hildegard was born in 1098, near Bingen in the Rhine River Valley in Germany, the tenth child of noble parents. A sickly girl, she began seeing visions at an early age. Hildegard's parents had dedicated her to God, and by the time she was eight, they brought her to the church to be raised by a spiritual woman named Jutta, an anchoress at the convent. Too ill to be a student, Hildegard absorbed the prayers and music of the religious life that now surrounded her. Other women came to the abbey to join Jutta in a life of religious devotion. After Jutta's death, Hildegard was elected abbess and served in that role for the rest of her life.

In 1141, Hildegard had a vision that led her to a new understanding of her purpose in life. In her words, "the heavens were opened and a blinding light of exceptional brilliance flowed through my entire brain." This powerful vision enabled her to understand the meaning of religious writings and commanded her to record everything that was revealed to her. A monk served as her secretary and wrote down Hildegard's visions and prophetic revelations.

Her unusual abilities attracted others to seek out Hildegard for advice and help for their needs. Some came to work and pray; others came for medical and spiritual guidance. In addition to her ministry to others, Hildegard produced major works related to theology, medicine, natural history, and music. When few women held positions of respect, she was consulted by and advised bishops, kings, and popes. In her pursuit of true piety, she built a new abbey to house the numbers of women who came to join her work. She also undertook four preaching journeys, the last one when she was well into her seventies.

Hildegard died near Bingen in 1179, at the age of eighty-one. Saint Hildegard's feast day is September 17.

Mission

Hildegard's passion was for living an interior life in the presence of God and for sharing her inner voice with God's church. While Hildegard never doubted that her visions were of divine origin, in humility, she was reluctant to share her prophetic wisdom with others until encouraged by church leaders to do so. She considered her response to God's will a simple abandonment, a soul held by God like a feather carried by the wind. However, when Saint Bernard of Clairvaux and Pope Eugenius endorsed her visions, Hildegard's mission to the church was born.

For ten years, she worked on her first book, *Scivias*, meaning, "Know the Ways." Once her writings were published, she became widely known in Germany and beyond. She corresponded at length with four popes, two emperors, King Henry II of England, and many other church leaders. She warned clergy to remain true to their vocation as spiritual leaders; she admonished civil rulers to remember to exercise their authority with justice. Not only through her writings, but also by her preaching, Hildegard proclaimed her prophetic message to nuns, monks, laity, priests, and bishops as she traveled throughout the Rhineland.

Legacy

Hildegard's life of justice and compassion form the basis of her legacy to the church today. Her pattern of combining contemplative prayer with an active pursuit of God's mission on earth offers modern day Christians a model of a balanced life. Unafraid to speak out, Hildegard called for justice and compassion in dealing with others, even risking her position as an abbess in defending those whom she believed had been condemned unfairly.

In addition to a spiritual legacy, Hildegard left behind a wealth of insight regarding healing and wellness for all of God's creation. Although her scientific works were written differently from her prophetic visions, they still reflected her spiritual belief that humans were the peak of God's creation, and that they were given the responsibility to use and care for God's world with reverence and wisdom.

The key to life in the spirit for Hildegard was music, the highest form of praise. Overall, she wrote at least seventy-seven songs and a liturgical drama. Hildegard composed hymns and sequences in honor of saints and Mary. Her songs share rich poetic images about the humanity of Jesus. To Hildegard, singing was praying, the highest form of reverence.

Hildegard represents the willingness to serve God with all the gifts one is given. Hildegard's example challenges everyone to affirm their own talents and skills and to respect their own experiences of God's presence, using it all to make a difference in the world.

Bodily/Kinesthetic Intelligence

Learn

By playing a game of charades, participants will communicate ideas about God's role in their lives through images inspired by the writings of Hildegard of Bingen.

Locate

3" x 5" index cards; Pens.

Advance Preparation

Prepare materials for a game of Charades by printing these phrases on separate 3" x 5" index cards:

God carries me like a . . . feather on the wind.
God challenges me like a . . . strong wave.
God cheers me like a . . . sunny day.
God cleanses me like a . . . bubble bath.
God corrects me like a . . . caring teacher.
God guides me like a . . . lighthouse.
God nurtures me like a . . . mother's touch.
God protects me like a . . . heavy shield.
God purifies me like a . . . refiner's fire.
God refreshes me like a . . . cold drink.
God supports me like a . . . strong arm.
God surrounds me like a . . . giant hug.

Lead

Hildegard's writing is filled with vivid imagery that communicates her understanding of God's presence in the life of faithful believers. She looked for ways to share her visions of God's power and work in creation and in her life. Trying to explain her mystic experiences of God's presence, she wrote: " . . . I raise my hands aloft to God, that I might be held by God, just like a feather which has no weight from its own strength and lets itself be carried by the wind."[5]

The image of being a "feather on the wind of God" captures our imaginations and helps us understand the way Hildegard abandoned herself to God's Spirit. As Christians today, we can learn from Hildegard the importance of sharing with others the experience of God's action in our lives. We, too, can create word pictures that communicate our faith.

Develop a game of charades to help the participants act out ideas about how God's presence influences their lives today. Begin by practicing with the prepared example from Hildegard: "God carries me like" . . . "a feather on the wind." Say the first part, and then ask the learners to act out the image of a feather on the wind. Explain that in charades the point of the game is to pantomime an idea so that others can guess the words. Divide the participants into groups or teams.

---

[5] Durka, Gloria. *Praying with Hildegard of Bingen*. Winona, MN: Saint Mary's Press, 1991, p. 33.

Distribute the prepared cards that have both a statement about God's action and a phrase that describes that activity. Instruct the players that they may say the first part, the verb phrase about God. Then they must act out the phrase that comes after "like a . . . " Give the teams a few moments to discuss how they could portray the suggested phrase. Then invite the groups to take turns acting out their word pictures about God. Give the team a point if the observers can guess the idea pantomimed. After playing charades with the suggested phrases, challenge the participants to create their own statements about God's action in their lives and continue playing the game.

Interpersonal Intelligence

Learn

By writing cinquain poetry, participants will affirm Hildegard's commitment to justice.

Locate

Paper; Pencils or pens.

Lead

For Hildegard, justice was a way of life. Hildegard believed that to be a spiritual person was to be in community, living in harmony with others, sharing and giving whatever was needed. This sense of justice formed the basis for Hildegard's expression of faith. She treated all those who sought her help with the same sense of dignity and compassion, whether they were poor or rich, anonymous, or famous. Always aware of the world around her and its needs, Hildegard acted to bring God's justice to situations and to creation. Her life is an inspiration to those who would choose to act justly in a complex world by boldly living a simple faith.

Ask the learners to name people they know or have heard about in the world today who follow Hildegard's example of pursuing justice. Their lists may include categories of justice-seekers such as parents, police officers, or teachers, or they may name specific individuals such as Martin Luther King, Jr., Oscar Romero, Jane Addams, or other modern champions of justice.

Explain that each pupil will write a poetic tribute to one person who exemplifies the meaning of justice. Demonstrate the process by using a five-line poetry pattern known as a "cinquain." The formula is:

Line One: A one-word noun.
Line Two: Two adjectives that describe the noun.
Line Three: Three "ing" words that describe the noun.
Line Four: Four words that express a feeling about the noun.
Line Five: One word that is a synonym for the noun.

Work together to create a cinquain based on Hildegard's life. For example:

Hildegard
Humble, Vibrant
Caring, Giving, Loving
Envisioning a just world
Champion.

Suggest that participants use this sample as a model for their own poems about people who seek justice today. Provide paper and pencils or pens and allow time for poets to work alone or in pairs. Invite the learners to read their cinquains to the group. Use these creative expressions to celebrate the work of justice among God's people.

Intrapersonal Intelligence

Learn

By decorating a candle with symbols and words related to the life of Saint Hildegard of Bingen, participants will remember her challenge to live a life of prayer in the light of God's presence.

Locate

Brushes; Candles, thick white approximately eight inches tall; Containers for glue; Glue; Matches; Permanent markers, fine-tipped; Scissors; Stickers with symbols of light; Tissue paper; Water.

Lead

God's inspiration and care often came to Hildegard as the image of light, a warming flame. She believed that Christians are called to be light to the world through the light of God. One of Hildegard's lessons is that prayer is the key to opening our lives to God's light.

In her Benedictine habit, Hildegard lived the monastic discipline of prayer, study, and work. Seven periods divided the day. The first began at 2 a.m.. with the chanting of *nocturnes*. After returning for a short sleep, the sisters rose before 6 a.m. to say *lauds*. After this, they spent time in private reading or meditation in their cells, and then returned to chapel to recite *prime*. After breakfast and chores, the sisters gathered to offer *terce* and to participate in the Eucharistic liturgy. The morning's work then followed with manual labor in the gardens or vineyards. Before noon, they prayed *sext*, and then ate lunch and rested briefly.

Around 3:00 P.M. they gathered to sing *none*, following which they worked at various duties. After a light supper and the chanting of *vespers*, the nuns read, studied, and meditated before ending their day by reciting *compline* together. By days' end, Hildegard and her sisters had worked about six hours, slept eight hours, and prayed together for three or four hours. The rest of the day had been spent in meditation, spiritual reading, and study. The goal was to live in harmony with God, humankind, and themselves.

In the spirit of Saint Hildegard, decorate candles and use them as a devotional tool for times of personal prayer. Demonstrate the process for the project. Select a thick white candle, eight inches tall. Choose a variety of symbols and words related to the life of Hildegard and to the symbol of light. Phrases could include God is Light, Light, Light of Life, Light of the World, Living Light, or Lord of Light. Use permanent markers to trace illustrations, phrases, and words onto tissue paper. Carefully tear or cut around the designs. Dilute glue with water and place it into a container. Working in small sections, brush the glue mixture onto the candle. Press a tissue paper piece over the glue and smooth the edges. Continue adding pieces to the candle, overlapping each one as it is attached. If young children are involved in the project, use stickers of images related to light such as candles, rays, and stars, and affix them to the candle.

Provide supplies and guide the group as each person contributes to one candle for the classroom or creates an individual project for personal use. Once the candles are completed, light the wicks and read passages from Hildegard's writing or from the Bible (e,g., Isaiah 9:2 and John 1:1-14).

Logical/Mathematical Intelligence

Learn

By playing a matching game, participants will discover more about the many roles that Saint Hildegard played during her lifetime.

Locate

Construction paper or index cards; Markers.

Advance Preparation

Prepare a set of game cards by printing each title related to Hildegard in capital letters on separate sheets of construction paper. Then write each descriptive phrase on a separate piece of construction paper. If there are many participants, prepare two or more games. However, be sure to keep the pairs together within a given game. Information to use includes:

Abbess	Director of a community of religious women
Counselor	Giver of advice and guidance
Environmentalist	Observer of nature and preserver of Creation
Healer	Proponent of natural medicines and prayer
Musician	Composer of spiritual hymns of praise
Mystic	Listener to the inner voice of God
Peacemaker	Builder of harmonious relationships
Preacher	Speaker for God's church and the faith
Prophet	Sharer of God's vision and preserver of Creation
Writer	Author of *Scivias* and other visionary works

Lead

Hildegard of Bingen wore many "hats" during her years. For someone cloistered away from the world, she was an active participant in life, sharing a variety of gifts and talents. Because of the multiple roles Hildegard experienced, many words may be used to describe this saint. Play a matching game, patterned after the game *Concentration*, to find out more about Hildegard and her mission.

To play the game, shuffle the cards and place them face down in a tiled pattern on a table or on the floor. Instruct the first player to turn two cards face up and to read each of them. If the words in capital letters match the description that has been revealed, the person takes the pair of cards and takes another turn. If the items do not match, they are placed face down again and the next person takes a turn. Play continues until all of the matches have been made. The winner is the player (or team) with the most sets of matched cards.

When the game is over, use the pictures as a bulletin board display or combine the papers to create a booklet that may be shared with other people.

Musical/Rhythmic Intelligence

Learn

By listening to recordings of Hildegard of Bingen's musical compositions, participants will share their response to the sounds and harmonies they hear through a creative writing experience.

Locate

CD or cassette player; Markers; Paper; Pencils or pens; Recordings of Hildegard of Bingen's music such as: "900 Years—Hildegard von Bingen/Sequentia," "Canticles of Ecstasy," "Celestial Light," "Luminous Spirit," "Symphony Spiritual," and "Von Bingen."

Lead

For Hildegard, music was the highest form of praise. She believed that singing brought harmony to the soul and to life. Her experience in the monastery prepared her musical ear as well as her spiritual nature and paved the way for her to become a composer. She composed more music than any woman previously had. Even though she received no formal training in music, her talent and motivation drove her to write at least seventy-seven chants and a musical drama, which she entitled "The Ritual of the Virtues." Hildegard combined all of her music into a cycle called "The Symphony of the Harmony of the Heavenly Revelations." In addition, those who have studied her writings say that Hildegard used music over three hundred times as a way to explain spiritual truths.

Hildegard believed that in singing and playing music, humans could integrate mind, heart, and body, which could heal discord on earth and celebrate the harmony of heaven. She understood that music was often the best path for redirecting human hearts toward heaven and human relationships toward unity. Her music still survives today as a testimony to her talent and a witness to the truth of her belief in its power to tune the human spirit.

After sharing information with the learners about Hildegard's music, play selections to accompany a creative writing experience. Remind the listeners that Hildegard believed in the power of music and words to restore the connection between humans and God. Distribute paper and markers, pencils, or pens to the participants and invite them to record their thoughts as they listen quietly to Hildegard's music. Ask them to consider how they would complete the phrase, "Music is. . . ." As they listen, they may record words and thoughts that come to their minds, or they may draw pictures that reflect the impressions the sounds make on their spirits. After all have had the opportunity to respond to the music, invite participants to share their ideas and reflections with one another.

Naturalist Intelligence

Learn

By using recyclable materials to create puppets, participants will share some of Hildegard's insights about the importance of caring for God's creation.

Locate

Chopsticks or dowel rods; Exacto knives; Fabric; Felt; Glue; Needles; Pantyhose; Plastic tubs; Polyfoam carpet pad; Scissors; Styrofoam ball; Thread; Trims; Yarn.

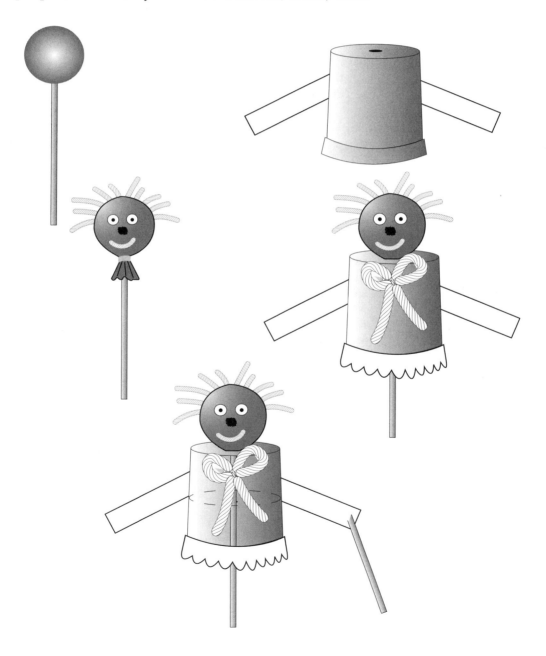

Lead

Hildegard believed that one of the best ways to know God was to appreciate "God's art," that is, all of Creation. She challenged everyone to live in awe of the majesty of God as revealed to us by the natural world. Hildegard taught that all of creation was precious and was a sacred trust from God to be cared for with love. Humans, she held, have a special responsibility to acknowledge God's presence in all living things.

One way to reverence God's presence in creation today is to make a commitment to care for the environment. Construct puppets from several recyclable objects. A Styrofoam ball forms the head, pantyhose becomes the skin, and a plastic margarine or frozen whipping cream tub serves as the shoulders. Strips of carpet pad turn into two arms and the chopstick or dowel rod becomes the stick by which the puppet is operated. Select characters to make such as Hildegard, one of her followers, an environmentalist, or a teacher. Then use the puppets to proclaim God's greatness by reading a Psalm, to tell Hildegard's story by using her words, or to educate others by sharing a message about stewardship of the earth.

Follow the step-by-step directions for making the rod puppet and demonstrate the process for the group. Insert the stick into the bottom of the Styrofoam ball. After the hole is made, remove the stick. Spread glue on both pieces, and re-insert the stick. Allow it to dry.

Cut a small hole into the bottom of the plastic tub. Also cut a small slit on each side of the container. The arms will be attached at these points. Cut arms from the polyfoam carpet pad and fit one into each side slit.

Cut a six-inch length of pantyhose. Tie off one of the loose ends, pull the section over the ball, and tie the piece around the stick with a strip of yarn. Using felt scraps, cut out eyes, nose and mouth. Glue them to the head. Choose yarn to make hair. Wrap it around the hand or a piece of cardboard several times. Snip open the ends, or leave them looped. Glue or sew the hair to the top of the head.

Insert the stick into the hole in the top of the plastic container. Pull the pantyhose through the hole, and tape them to the stick.

Choose fabric for the costume. Cut a hole into the center of it, and slide it over the puppet's head. Sew the material tightly around the neck. Make a few stitches on each side of the piece underneath the puppet's arms. Add trims to complete the costume.

Insert the other chopstick or another piece of dowel rod into a slit in one of the puppet's hands. To operate the character, hold the stick under the costume in one hand, and work the stick on the arm with the other hand.

Distribute materials and guide the puppet making process. When the characters are complete, take turns sharing information and insight about God's creation. Read Scripture passages such as Psalm 8, 19, 65:9-10, or 111:1-4. Or, recite a quote from Hildegard's writings such as "God wants the divine power to be manifested in all created forms because they are divine works." Finally, discuss the importance of recycling and the ways the students can participate in the effort.

Verbal/Linguistic Intelligence

Learn

By experiencing a first-person narrative, participants will comprehend biographical information regarding Saint Hildegard of Bingen and connect the events of her life to a related Bible story, Luke 10:38-42 and John 11:17-45, and to the importance of putting God at the center of their own lives.

Locate

Bible; Costume for "Nun" Storyteller; Story Script.

Lead

Share the story of Saint Hildegard of Bingen and tell the related Bible story of Martha and Mary as a first-person narrative. To enhance learning and to make the story memorable, a nun in traditional habit should relate memories about her favorite saint, Hildegard.

"Nun" Story Script
(adapted from Luke 10:38-42 & John 11:17-45)

Guten tag! That's German for "good day!" You would think that being from Germany, I would have a good German-sounding name; but no, my mother named me for a place she read about in the Bible. My name is Bethany; actually I am Sister Bethany. I have been a nun in the abbey here for many years. I am told that Bethany as a name means "life." I like that idea. I have devoted my life to God's work, and God's work has been my life.

God has been very good to me. It has been my good fortune to work closely with one of God's special people. Perhaps you have heard of Hildegard? My life has been closely entwined with hers these last few years as she attempts to do what God commands. If you know her story, you understand that she is a prophetic voice for God. Sister Hildegard sees visions and hears God's voice. When she is quiet and listening, her face seems transformed. She is transported to worlds the rest of us can only imagine. Then when she begins to speak about what she has seen and heard, it is my job to write down word-for-word the ideas God has given her. Sometimes I feel as if I am in the presence of God, too, as I record the visions Hildegard describes.

However, Hildegard is not always meditating and dreaming in a world of her own. At times, she is so busy and active that I can barely keep up. We write letters to great people of the world—even to the pope himself. We travel throughout Germany as Hildegard preaches about justice and the mission of God's church. When we are here, not only must Hildegard oversee the running of the convent, she also counsels the many people who show up to receive help with both physical and spiritual matters. This saintly person is constantly searching for cures in nature, and challenges us all to care for God's earth in our everyday living.

When I watch her work and pray, I sometimes feel as if I see two different people. The contemplative one who sits at the throne of God listening for the message of faith to share; and the dynamic one who seems bent on changing the world single-handedly!

Seeing Hildegard both work and pray, I am reminded of the Bible story of two sisters named Mary and Martha. Mary chose to sit at the feet of Jesus listening to his every word while Martha was the doer, the one who worked in the kitchen to feed the hungry disciples. It is as though Hildegard contains the qualities of both Mary and Martha in one soul! Interestingly enough, Mary and Martha lived in the little town outside Jerusalem named Bethany. Perhaps my mother was a little prophetic herself.

All I know is that Hildegard's passion for God's work has given me a model for the way to live as a Christian: it is not *either* prayer or work—it is a balance of both. From Hildegard, we learn the secret to making the most of each day: Put God at the center of whatever you do, and your life will have true meaning!

Visual/Spatial Intelligence

Learn

By creating art projects called *mandalas*, participants will recall Hildegard's visual expressions of prayer.

Locate

Crayons; Cardboard circles (e.g., cake or pizza rounds) or white drawing paper; Talcum powder or chalk dust; black tempera paint; Paper clips; Scissors.

Lead

Hildegard of Bingen created many beautiful works of art to express her beliefs as well as her visions. Many of her drawings were in the form of mandalas, circular shapes filled with geometric designs, as though one were looking at the universe. These art expressions were often created as a visible prayer, in response to music suitable to inspire reflection and worship. Interestingly, the mandala appears across many cultures as an almost mystical celebration of life and human experience. Today artists still use the concept of the mandala as an expression of the wholeness of life and the interrelatedness of all of creation.

Involve the participants in creating their own mandalas in response to the story of Hildegard. To begin, distribute large, circular shapes of white drawing paper or consider using cardboard circles, such as cake or pizza rounds, for the base of the art project. Direct the group to use crayons to fill the entire circle with multiple colors, pressing firmly and using bold strokes. When the paper or cardboard is completely coated with wax, have them lightly cover the drawing with talcum powder or chalk dust so that the paint will adhere to the surface. Mix black tempera paint according to directions, or use the pre-mixed liquid type, and add a squirt of dishwashing soap for easy clean-up. Next let the participants brush the entire surface of the paper with black paint. Allow the paint to dry. Give each person a scraping tool such as the point of a pair of scissors or the tip of an open paper clip to use to etch shapes and designs into the mandala.

Play recordings of Hildegard's music in the background (see page 150 for examples of recordings) as the learners work to create an expression of their own prayerful inner visions for God's world. Remind the students of Hildegard's words, "Creation reveals the hidden God."

OCTOBER
SAINT FRANCIS OF ASSISI

Biography

Saint Francis was born in Assisi, Italy, in 1181 or 1182, the son of wealthy cloth merchant Pietro Bernardone and his wife, Pica. They named their son Giovanni, but his father called him "Francesco" because the child was born while he was in France on business. Francis lived a life of luxury before entering the army. He was notorious for his frivolous lifestyle until 1203, when, during a battle between Assisi and Perugia, Francis was taken prisoner. After he was finally released, he returned home in poor health. In 1206, while praying at San Damiano, a local church, Francis felt the call of God on his life. The church being in disrepair, Francis sold some bolts of fabric belonging to his father and used the money to rebuild the structure. When Pietro discovered his son's actions, he beat Francis and demanded that he return the money, finally bringing him before the bishop.

For Francis, this was the final straw in his troubled relationship with his father. In his public humiliation, Francis threw the money on the ground, stripped the clothes from his body, and gave them to his father, announcing that he no longer wanted to be his father's son. A priest covered Francis with a laborer's robe, and that simple garment became the type of clothing Saint Francis wore for the rest of his life. The robe, cut in the shape of a cross, symbolized being a "laborer" for God and became the official garb of the Franciscan brothers.

Francis was determined to follow Christ's example, and he became known as "Poverello"—the "little poor one." Others began to join Francis in the life of poverty, traveling from place to place, sleeping out of doors, begging for food, preaching about God's loving care, and gently persuading people to rely on God and to care for one another. Francis focused on following Christ completely, finding joy in God's creation, and accepting sacrifice and suffering in order to change the world. So deep was his commitment to Christ that in 1224, he experienced the Stigmata, the appearance on his own body of the nail and sword wounds of Jesus. Francis died on October 4, 1226.

Mission

Although Francis only lived twenty years after his conversion, his life mission left an indelible mark. Francis had a passion for rebuilding Christ's church. At first he thought God was calling him to physically rebuild San Damiano, but then he came to see that his mission was broader: He was to challenge the church to have the courage to take the words of the gospel literally, to care for the poor and downtrodden. Francis worked with the poorest and most despised members of society, including the lepers. Although his life was one of poverty, Saint Francis lived in joy; his gentle good humor and sensitivity to all of creation drew others to share in his mission of spreading the gospel.

Legacy

Because Saint Francis was more concerned with actions than words, he did not leave behind many writings. However, several stories of the life of Saint Francis have been passed to us, preserving the legacy of a man who preferred to live the life of faith more than preach about it. Obviously Francis communicated clearly to others the message he had received from God because so many chose to follow his example and accept his challenge of a life of persistent self-sacrifice. The greatest testimony of the power of his life are the three Orders of Saint Francis that still exist today. The First Order was established for the men—the "little brothers"—who wanted to follow Francis' example. In less than three years, his order was multiplied to sixty monasteries. In 1212, Francis gave his habit to Clare, who founded the Second Order for women. Finally, Francis established the Third order for lay people who had a job and a family, yet wanted to be a part of his work to save the world by living in Christ's name. Another lasting gift of Saint Francis is found in prayers that he composed. "The Canticle of the Sun" celebrates the unity of all Creation and is a hymn of praise still sung to this day. His famous "Peace Prayer" reflects Francis' belief that words help shape our deeds. Francis' words still challenge us to live lives of peace.

Bodily/Kinesthetic Intelligence

Learn

By celebrating the joy of simplicity through expressive movement, participants will experience the lessons taught by Saint Francis for a sufficient and satisfying life.

Locate

Cassette tape or CD of "Simple Gifts" (instrumental arrangement of Shaker melodies available at www.simpleliving.org); Cassette tape or CD player; Resources on the Shaker tradition.

Advance Preparation

Obtain information on the Shakers. Use resources from the Internet or library. Or, contact:

Shaker Town
3500 Lexington Road
Pleasant Hill, KY 40330
(502) 734-5411

Lead

Saint Francis did not consider his life to be one of misery and sacrifice, but rather a life lived in the joy of close dependency on God. Living simply is not easy. We are pressured by society to accept the world's definition of what is "enough," which, of course, is never fully achieved. However, Saint Francis challenges us to follow Jesus' example of seeing life as an opportunity to give, rather than a chance to get. Those who look for ways to care for others and live nearer to God's reality are those who find true wealth and satisfaction in life. Simplicity brings great rewards, not by what we possess, but by what possesses us: a passion to do more with less, to live nearer life's central purpose, and to keep our priorities clear and our hearts pure.

Engage the participants in a discussion of what simplicity means. Brainstorm ideas and make lists of life's simple pleasures. Suggest that some of the gifts we often overlook include joys like: time with our families, sunshine and blue skies, love of friends and pets, and smiles and hugs. Connect their ideas with the teachings of Saint Francis. Tell of Francis' love for all of creation as a gift from God. Review his choices about living simply by faith, depending on God to provide for his basic needs of life.

Explain that the learners will be using their bodies to express the joy we feel when we celebrate the simple gifts life has to offer. Share information about a religious group known as the Shakers and the simple lifestyle that they lived. Tell the students that the Shakers were a people who sought peace, justice, and equality not only for themselves, but also for others.

One of the most famous Shaker songs is "Simple Gifts." Movements were added to the music and the words, and it was used as a dance. The shaking hands signified shedding tensions and evils and the gathering in, or scooping, symbolized receiving God's blessings. Invite the children to try this dance as an expression of Saint Francis' commitment to living a life of simplicity.

Form a circle and instruct each child to find a partner. Use the following movements to interpret each phrase of the song.

'Tis the gift to be simple, 'tis the gift to be free,
'Tis the gift to come down where we ought to be,
(Move to the center of the circle holding arms in front, elbows bent, and with relaxed wrists,

shake hands.)

And when we find ourselves in the place just right,
'Twill be in the valley of love and delight.
(Move back and re-form the circle, with arms still extended in front, but with palms up in a scooping gesture.)

When true simplicity is gained,
To bow and to bend we shan't be ashamed.
(Face partner and bow.)

To turn, turn will be our delight.
(Turn and bow to person on the other side.)

'Til by turning, turning we come round right.
(Turn in place. End facing the center so the dance may be repeated.)

Conclude the activity by encouraging the participants to put Saint Francis' example of simplicity into practice.

Interpersonal Intelligence

Learn

By working together to dramatize the Christmas story, participants will recall Saint Francis' legend associated with the crèche.

Locate

Bibles; Costumes for Christmas story characters; Paper; Pencils or pens.

Lead

A legend is told that in 1223, Saint Francis re-created the events of Christ's birth with a live nativity scene in the hills near Assisi, Italy. After he filled a manger with hay, surrounded it with real animals, and placed a wax image of the Baby Jesus into the crib, Francis re-told the Christmas story to the villagers and the shepherds.

In the spirit of Saint Francis, experience the story of the Nativity through the use of drama. Create an easy script from the words of the scripture passage, Luke 2:1-20, by following four simple steps. The goal is to break the Bible verses into character parts so that the passage will be more understandable to those hearing it. The object is not to embellish the text and to add details that are not suggested, but to adhere as closely as possible to the words of the Bible. Review the four steps.

Step 1.

Identify the characters in the passage and make a list of these people.

Step 2.

Find all of the quotes in the passage. Match a character to each of them. Write the person's name on the left side of a paper, and write the words of the quote next to it. Try to break long passages into several parts.

Step 3.

Write lines for any portion of the passage that could be assigned to a specific person. Clues to look for are verbs. These words suggest that the narrative could be written in dialogue form.

Step 4.

Add a narrator, or several, to provide information between the speaking parts.

A sample script, based on Luke 2:1-20, is provided. Use it as the text for the drama activity or have the participants follow the four "Scripture Script" steps to create their own version of the story. Then invite the children to take turns playing the parts: narrator, Caesar Augustus, Joseph, Mary, angels and shepherds. Drape pieces of fabric over the actors' heads and shoulders to create simple costumes.

Sample Script

Caesar Augustus: A census must be taken of the entire Roman world. Everyone must go to his or her own town to register.

Joseph: Mary, we must go from Nazareth to Bethlehem, because I am of the house and line of David.

Mary: It will be a long journey for me since my baby is due to be born very soon.

Narrator: Upon arriving in Bethlehem, Joseph and Mary discovered that there was no room for them in the inn.

Joseph: We will stay in the stable where the cattle are kept.

Narrator: While they were there, the time came for the baby to be born, and Mary gave birth to her firstborn, a son.

Mary: Let us wrap the baby in cloths to keep him warm.

Joseph: We can place him in the manger.

Narrator: There were shepherds living out in the fields nearby, keeping watch over their flocks.

Shepherd One: Look (with scared expression), this angel of the Lord appears to us, and the glory of the Lord shines around us.

Angel: Do not be afraid, I bring you good news of great joy that will be for all the people. Today in the town of David, a Savior has been born to you; he is Christ the Lord. This will be a sign to you: You will find a baby wrapped in cloths and lying in a manger.

Shepherd Two: Wow! (pointing skyward) Look at that! A great company of the heavenly host is with the angel, praising God. What are they saying?

Angels: Glory to God in the highest, and on earth peace to men on whom his favor rests.

Narrator: When the angels returned to heaven, the shepherds said to one another:

Shepherd One: Let's go to Bethlehem and see this thing that has happened, which the Lord has told us about.

Shepherd Two: (at the manger, kneeling) It is a baby in the manger.

Shepherd One: (kneeling) Let us worship him. Then we must spread the word concerning what has been told to us about this child.

Shepherd Two: All who hear what we tell them will be amazed.

Mary: And I, too, will treasure all of these things and ponder them in my heart.

Narrator: The shepherds returned, glorifying and praising God for all that they had heard and seen, which were just as they had been told.

Intrapersonal Intelligence

Learn

By adding movement to Saint Francis' "Peace Prayer," participants will use the words as a catalyst for exploring their roles as peacemakers in the world.

Locate

Paper or newsprint; Pencils, pens, or markers.

Lead

"Lord, make me an instrument of your peace . . . " are the familiar words that begin the "Peace Prayer" of Saint Francis of Assisi. Read the inspiring lines to the participants.

> Lord, make me an instrument of your peace.
> Where there is hatred, let me sow love,
> Where there is injury, pardon,
> Where there is darkness, light,
> Where there is sadness, joy,
> Where there is doubt, faith,
> And where there is despair, hope.
>
> O Divine Master,
> Grant that I may not so much seek
> To be consoled as to console,
> To be understood as to understand,
> To be loved as to love.
> For it is in giving that we receive,
> It is in pardoning that we are pardoned,
> And it is in dying that we are born to eternal life.

Invite the class to add movements and gestures to the words to better express their meaning. Take turns having different students interpret each phrase with their choice of a movement or gesture.

Then have the learners re-write Saint Francis' thoughts using their own words to form prayers. Instruct the pupils to focus on ways that they can be peacemakers in the family, parish, school, neighborhood, community, state, nation, and world. Share examples such as:

> Lord, make me an instrument of your peace.
> Where there is arguing,
> Let me bring problem solving.
>
> Lord, make me an instrument of your peace.
> Where there is name calling,
> Let me bring kind words.

Distribute paper and pencils or pens to individuals, or use a chalkboard and chalk or newsprint and markers for groups. Guide the class as they compose personal peace prayer phrases. Invite the students to share their writings. Also, encourage them to interpret the personal peace prayers through movement and gesture as before.

Logical/Mathematical Intelligence

Learn

By creating "building blocks" and cooperating to construct a symbolic wall, learners will connect stories from Saint Francis' life with his mission for rebuilding the church.

Locate

Bible; Cardboard bricks, cartons, or shoe boxes; Glue; Markers or crayons; Newsprint sheets, large paper grocery bags; Poster paints; Paint brushes; Scissors; Tape.

Lead

As a young man, Francis grew in spiritual strength as he sought God's will for his life. One day he was kneeling before the altar in the church of Saint Damiano, just outside the walls of Assisi, Italy. As he looked up at the crucifix, the figure of Christ seemed to say to him: "Francis, go and repair my church which you see is falling into ruins." Francis understood this command to mean that he was physically to rebuild Saint Damiano, and he set about finding ways to raise money for his mission, even selling goods that belonged to his father. This made his father Pietro Bernardone angry and resulted in Francis leaving his father's house and embracing a life of poverty. When finished repairing Saint Damiano, Francis moved down the hill to work on a little chapel called Saint Mary of the Portiuncula. Ultimately, Francis realized that although several physical church buildings needed attention, so did the universal church, the people called the Body of Christ. Francis gathered around him a small group of followers committed to the gospel message of healing the sick, feeding the hungry, protecting the poor, and confronting all evil. Thus, Saint Francis and his "little brothers" set about rebuilding the church, not by using brick and mortar, but by imitating Jesus.

During Francis' lifetime, the church was in need of rebuilding, but that is true in every generation. Ask the participants to brainstorm the "constructive building materials" that would help restore the Body of Christ, the church, today. Suggestions for positive values might include: acceptance, caring, cooperation, gentleness, honesty, joy, kindness, love, openness, sharing, and trust. The list of positive ideas is endless. Tell the students they will be making building blocks and using these values to illustrate the call to renew and restore God's church in every age.

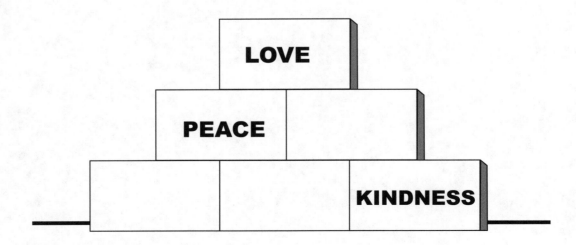

Distribute the cardboard bricks, cartons, or shoe boxes. Provide materials such as newsprint sheets and paper grocery bags as well as paints and brushes, markers, scissors, glue and tape. Direct the group to cover the bricks with paper or paint. Then have each student choose positive words to print on each side of the brick. After the construction process is completed, have the participants cooperate to build a wall, turning the bricks to display the words they wish to emphasize as a prayer for God's church.

Conclude the activity by reading 1 Peter 2:4-5 to the group. Challenge the listeners to be "living stones" of the church in God's world.

Musical/Rhythmic Intelligence

Learn

By hearing the story of the hymn, "All Creatures of Our God and King," and creating dioramas to remember the message, participants will appreciate Saint Francis' prayer, "Canticle of the Sun."

Locate

Construction paper, light blue and dark blue or black; Fabric scraps; Glue; Markers; Music for "All Creatures of Our God and King"; Natural objects like grass, flowers, leaves, pebbles, or pine cones; Pipe cleaners; Scissors; Shoe boxes; Wooden clothespins with rounded tops; Yarn.

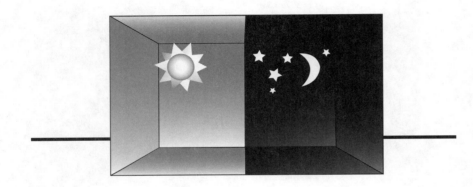

Advance Preparation

Create a diorama as the visual aid for telling the story of Saint Francis' hymn, "All Creatures of Our God and King." In advance or during the storytelling, form the background by covering a shoe box with construction paper. Inside the box, cover half with light blue and half with dark blue or black to suggest day and night. To decorate the inside, draw, cut from paper, or purchase stickers (sun, moon, stars) that suggest the elements of nature honored in the song. Another option is to include real specimens of nature in the diorama.

In addition, a small figure can be added to the scene, representing Saint Francis. Draw a face on one side of the rounded top of a clothespin. Twist a pipe cleaner around the neck to form arms. Cut a two-inch by six-inch rectangle of fabric. Fold it in half and cut a small slit in the center. Slide the head through the opening. Arrange the material over the arms. Secure it in place by tying a piece of yarn around the middle. Use yarn glued to the top of the clothespin for hair, gluing it in a circle to create a "bald spot" for Francis.

Lead

Some of Saint Francis' most beautiful words, "The Canticle of the Sun," have been set to music and are sung as a hymn called "All Creatures of Our God and King." Locate the song in a hymnal or play a recording of the music and the words. Share the story of the song, which was written approximately eight hundred years ago. Use the following script as a guide for discussion and create the diorama as a teaching tool while sharing the story.

Story Script

Let's put the background on our diorama while we learn the background of the story of the hymn, "All Creatures of Our God and King." The man who wrote this hymn, Saint Francis of Assisi, was the son of a wealthy family in Italy, and grew up very spoiled and privileged. Then, Francis discovered the joy of giving to the poor and serving the Son of God. All of his life, Saint Francis found God's presence in the beauty of nature around him. He called the sun his brother. (Hold up the model sun you have chosen as the story is told.) The first thing to put in our diorama is the sun to remind us that Saint Francis was the *son* of a wealthy cloth merchant, a follower of the *Son* of God, and a man who saw the beauty of God's creation in his brother, the *sun*. In fact, another name for this hymn is "Canticle of the Sun."

Like all creatures on earth, Saint Francis did not always have sunny, easy days. Some times were dark and difficult for Francis. Of the many prayers he wrote, Saint Francis composed this hymn toward the end of his life when he was sick and nearly blind. Yet even then he found joy in the gifts of creation, like his Sister Moon and Brother Fire who give light in the darkness. (Place the moon and stars on the "night" side of the diorama.)

As Saint Francis traveled with his friends, he saw all of creation as symbols of love: God's love for us and our love for God. What favorite parts of creation represent God's love to you? Flowers? Trees? Grass? Saint Francis saw these gifts of nature as our most precious possessions; he chose to live without money, to live simply, and to take care of the poor. It made Saint Francis sad when the noblest creatures—humans—failed to praise God. (Add nature artifacts or cut outs to represent the joy of creation in the diorama. Also, add the figure of Saint Francis to the scene.)

As we sing "All Creatures of our God and King," we should remember how important it is to praise the God of creation. In the beauty of this season, we should listen and observe Saint Francis' words: "Let all things their Creator bless . . . Alleluia!"

After sharing the story of the song, invite the participants to create their own dioramas to remember the message of the music. Provide supplies and guide the process as explained in "Advance Preparation." Display the completed projects for others to enjoy.

Naturalist Intelligence

Learn

By creating edible decorations to hang in trees for the birds, participants will demonstrate the lessons Francis taught about the special role humans have in caring for creation.

Locate

Birdseed; Bread cubes; Cranberries; Floral wire; Grapefruit or orange halves; Illustration of Saint Francis and the birds (optional); Knives; Peanut butter; Pipe cleaners; Popcorn; Pretzel sticks or twists; Raisins; Scissors; Suet.

Lead

For Saint Francis of Assisi, all of creation was a proclamation of God's goodness and love. He taught that, "We are sister and brother to animals and plants, water and soil, earth and sky." In fact, Saint Francis always referred to elements of creation with family terms such as, "Brother Sun," "Mother Earth," or "Sister Moon."

One story from Saint Francis' life tells of his special relationship with the birds. This story relates that as he was traveling, Francis noticed a large flock of birds. Leaving his companions, he moved eagerly toward his feathered friends, who seemed to be waiting for him. He began talking to them: "Brother birds, you ought to praise and love your Creator very much. He has given you feathers for clothing, wings for flying, and everything you need. He has made you the noblest of his creatures, for he has appointed the pure air for your habitation." The birds reportedly began to sing and rejoice, responding to Francis as he moved among them, stroking them with the fringe of his tunic.

This story of Saint Francis encourages us to remember the special relationship humans have with creation. The flight and song of the birds reminds us of the freedom and joy God's love offers to us. Invite the participants to celebrate the spirit of Saint Francis by designing ways to care for our feathered friends, the birds.

Offer the participants an opportunity to decorate a "wildlife tree" with attractive, edible gifts for our brothers and sisters in creation, the birds. Explain that, especially in winter, birds struggle to find enough to eat; they especially need fat and seeds to survive. Invite the group to make decorations like birdseed pretzels, fruit baskets, and popcorn strings. Demonstrate the process to create each project.

For birdseed pretzels, tie a loop of string or yarn through the top of a large pretzel stick or a pretzel twist. Cover the pretzel with peanut butter and roll it in birdseed. Hang it on the limb of a tree. To create fruit baskets, fill empty grapefruit or orange halves with a combination of bread cubes, mixed seeds, and suet chunks. Attach pipe cleaners at three places around the edge of the fruit; join them at the center and twist to form a hook to use to hang the feeder on branches. In addition, string popcorn, as well as cranberries and raisins on pieces of floral wire. Bend the wire and attach the ends to form a circle that can be hung over the ends of the branches.

Provide the supplies and guide the group as they create edible gifts for Saint Francis' friends, the birds. As a group, hang the projects on a tree on the church or school property, or allow each person to take his or her creations home to share with feathered friends in their own neighborhood.

Verbal/Linguistic Intelligence

Learn

By experiencing a first-person narrative, participants will comprehend biographical information regarding Saint Francis of Assisi and connect the events of his life to a related Bible story, Matthew 19:16-26, and to the importance of choosing to follow Christ.

Locate

Bible; Costume for "Franciscan Brother" Storyteller; Story script.

Lead

Share the story of Saint Francis of Assisi and tell the related Bible story as a first-person narrative. To enhance learning and to make the story memorable, a costumed "Franciscan brother" should relate memories about his favorite saint, Francis.

"Franciscan Brother" Story Script
(adapted from Matthew 19:16-26)

The Lord give you peace! I am Giovanni, a Franciscan brother. I have not always been as you see me today. Now I am dressed in a simple habit and travel barefoot, but once I dressed in the latest fashions and lived a life of wealth and ease. Do you think that made me happy? I can tell you it did not. Then one day, I heard the story of another man named "Giovanni." Like me, he had grown up in a rich family with every opportunity and advantage. Then he discovered that true wealth came from knowing God's love. You may know "Giovanni" better by his nickname, "Francis." You may even call him Saint Francis of Assisi. He began our order by following the command of Christ to "go forth and spread the gospel," trusting God in all things.

When I first heard about Saint Francis, I admired him very much. I decided that I wanted to become a brother and find this happiness for myself. I left the comforts of my home, took a vow of poverty, and now live freely, finding my joy in the beauty of God's world all around me. I am a rich man.

What do you think it means to be rich? To have great wealth and own a big house? Saint Francis would disagree. He was inspired by the gospel story of Jesus and the rich, young ruler. In this story, a young man comes to Jesus wanting to be "perfect," to be good enough to have eternal life. He tells Jesus that he has always done what was right and has kept the commandments. Jesus looks into his heart and knows this person's need. Jesus tells him to sell everything he owns and give it to the poor; then he can come and follow Jesus. The young man's eager face fell. He had many possessions, and he couldn't part with what he thought made him happy.

Saint Francis decided to make a different choice than the rich, young ruler. He gave up everything that the world calls "riches," and discovered in his poverty that God's loving presence is worth more than money or houses. We Franciscans understand that the truly poor are those who do not know God. This is my message to you: be wiser than the rich, young ruler. We must let nothing stand in the way of our knowing God's love. If you choose to follow Christ, then you will have a life rich with a joy that possesses you.

Visual/Spatial Intelligence

Learn

By creating and using puppets to represent "people of peace," learners will be able to act out peace-making strategies like those used by Saint Francis and his followers.

Locate

Bibles; Duct tape; Fabric; Felt; Glue; Paper towel tubes; Plastic bottles from dish washing soap or laundry detergent; Scissors; Yarn, fake fur, or Fiberfil.

Advance Preparation

In advance, wash the bottles, remove the labels, and dry the containers.

Lead

Saint Francis believed that followers of Christ must be people of peace. He took seriously the command of Jesus to heal the sick and to take God's peace everywhere in the world. He opposed the Crusades (Christian military efforts to re-take the Holy Land from the Muslims) of his own day and traveled to speak to Muslims of the love of God and the peace of Christ. Saint Francis saw God's image in all of creation, especially in the faces of God's people. He taught his followers to view all things in the world as gifts of God, owning nothing, and thanking God for everything.

Share the Scripture passage—Matthew 10:7-13—which served as an inspiration on Saint Francis' life to live as a person of peace. Discuss the ideas in the passage that Saint Francis made specific requirements for those in his order: accepting Christ's command to preach the Gospel, traveling with only bare essentials, speaking peace to everyone, staying with those who offer welcome. Conclude with Saint Francis' teaching that Christ's followers must be "people of peace." Explain that the participants will explore ways to live out that message by creating "puppets of peace."

Next, invite the participants to read Matthew 25:34-40. Ask how the "righteous" who sit on the right hand of God are like those Saint Francis called "people of peace." Discuss what actions reveal their inner beliefs. Suggest that the learners make puppets that represent the "people of peace" and act out ways that the hungry can be fed, the thirsty given drink, the stranger welcomed, the poor clothed, the sick visited, or the imprisoned ministered to.

Help each child pick a person of peace to create. It could be a biblical, historical or contemporary figure including people such as Jane Addams, Clara Barton, Tom Dooley, Martin Luther King, Jr., Rosa Parks, Mother Teresa, or Sojourner Truth. It could also depict Saint Francis or one of his followers or it could represent the puppet maker. If necessary, find information about these people of peace in books, magazines, newspapers, recordings, Internet, and other sources. Then report his or her story by making and using a bottle puppet.

Used bottles, in various shapes and sizes, can be recycled into puppets by adding low-cost or no-cost materials. Provide a plastic dishwashing soap or laundry detergent bottle for each child. To make the puppets, turn the bottles upside down and decide if the part with the handle will form the front or the back of the face. If it is to be the front, the handle becomes the puppet's nose. Distribute paper towel tubes and pieces of duct tape. Place a paper towel tube on the pouring spout of the bottle. It will become the rod by which the puppet is operated. Use duct tape to secure the two pieces together. Make felt scraps available, as well as scissors, and give the children an opportunity to form the face. Ask them to cut eyes and a mouth and to glue them in place. Eyebrows, eyelashes, and cheeks may also be added.

Show the children how to make hair from yarn, fake fur, or Fiberfil. Guide them in this process and help them glue the hair to the top of the puppet's head.

Invite each person to choose a large square of fabric for the costume. Tell them to cut a small hole in the center of the material and to slide their paper towel tube through it. The fabric is taped to the neck of the puppet. Contrasting pieces and trims may complete the costume.

Give each child a turn to tell the story of his or her person of peace. Conclude the activity by asking each person to make a commitment to promote peace and to live the message of Matthew 25 in his or her own place in God's world.

NOVEMBER
SAINT MARGARET OF SCOTLAND

Biography

Margaret of Scotland (c. 1045-1093), as one of the last members of the Anglo-Saxon royal family, had to flee England after the Norman conquest of 1066. When her ship was blown off course, Margaret and her family were welcomed in Scotland by King Malcolm. Malcolm fell in love with the beautiful, refined Margaret who represented a striking contrast to the rough culture of the warring clans of the Scots. She had been well educated in Hungary where her family had been exiled during the rule of Danish kings in England and had intended to enter a convent to pursue the spiritual life. When Malcolm convinced her to marry him, Margaret brought her love of learning, manners, and virtue to her adopted homeland.

Margaret taught Malcolm to love justice and mercy and to spend much time in prayer. Although he could not read himself, Malcolm valued Margaret's books. If he knew Margaret particularly delighted in one, he would have the volume decorated with gold and gems.

Margaret encouraged other countries to bring heretofore unknown precious goods to Scotland and quietly introduced European culture to the court in Dunfermline. She founded monasteries, churches, and hostels for pilgrims, and helped to reform the church in Scotland. Margaret also won the respect and love of ordinary people with her generosity and genuine caring. She was always helping the poor and homeless, even before she cared for herself.

Margaret and Malcolm had eight children, two girls and six boys. Three of them became Scotland's noblest kings, and collectively their reigns were known as "The Golden Age" of Scotland. Margaret died four days after learning of her husband's and son's death in battle. Her daughter Maud married Stephen, king of England, and it is through her line that the present British royal family trace their descent from the earliest Anglo-Saxon Kings of England.

Saint Margaret's feast day is celebrated on November 16.

Mission

Margaret demonstrated in her own life the loving pattern of the Savior whom she worshipped. She kept her priorities clear: first prayer, then caring for others, and lastly attending to her own needs. Margaret fed orphans by her own hand, washed the feet of the poor, and raided the royal treasury to help the poor and homeless because she saw in the faces of the needy the face of Christ. Her devotion to the church led her to establish a workshop in her own quarters where a guild of noble ladies decorated vestments with silk and golden thread. Stories of her generosity and acts of mercy abound in historical accounts of her life.

Legacy

Margaret is one of the few saints to be a member of the laity and one of an even fewer number who was married and had children. Her religious example and good influence were felt not only in her own family, but in all of Scotland. Even though only one person, her loving acts affected a whole country and changed human history. Through stories of her acts of charity and loving devotion to God, her example reaches to everyone who is seeking to know Christ today.

Bodily/Kinesthetic Intelligence

Learn

By retelling a Bible story, John 13:4-17, participants will understand the importance that Jesus, as well as Saint Margaret of Scotland, placed on serving others.

Locate

"Jesus Serves" Action Story Script.

Lead

Saint Margaret of Scotland's life provides the example that in accepting Christ's sacrifice for us, we are able to sacrifice for others. Although Margaret was a queen, was wealthy, and had a loving family—a husband and eight children—she knew that her life was only complete by putting Christ first and by serving others in Jesus' name. In John 13:4-17, Jesus demonstrated this important theme when he washed the feet of his disciples. Saint Margaret took this Bible lesson to heart, as she showed God's love in this same manner to many people in her kingdom.

As an engaging method of teaching Jesus' followers today about Saint Margaret's commitment to service, invite the participants to share in retelling the Bible story of Jesus washing the disciples' feet by acting out the passage together. Explain that in an action story the leader says a line and demonstrates the motions, and the participants repeat the words and the gestures.

"Jesus Serves" Action Story Script
(adapted from John 13:4-17)

Jesus rose from supper.
(Stand up.)

Tied a towel around his waist.
(Pantomime tying towel around waist.)

Poured water in a basin.
(Pantomime pouring water from pitcher into bowl.)

Knelt and washed his helpers' feet.
(Kneel on one knee and pantomime washing someone's feet.)

Then Jesus challenged his disciples.
(Stand and gesture with index finger toward others.)

"Do as I have done to you."
(Point to self then others.)

"Live a life of loving service."
(Cross arms over chest.)

"Follow me in all you do."
(Extend arms in front of body.)

Interpersonal Intelligence

Learn

By playing a game of "Mirror, Mirror," participants will demonstrate Margaret's pattern of following Jesus' example of service to others.

Locate

Bowls; Cups; Knives; Marmalade; Napkins; Pitchers; Plates; Shortbread cookies; Spoons; Trays; Water.

Lead

Saint Margaret was a princess who planned to give her life to the church. In 1066, when she fled England, her ship was blown off course, bringing her to Scotland where King Malcolm fell in love with her beauty and grace. When they married, Margaret became Queen of Scotland and was deeply loved by the Scottish people, especially as she mirrored Christ's love in her life.

Play a game of "Mirror, Mirror" to demonstrate this theme. Have the participants choose partners and stand facing each other. Explain that one person will be the leader and the other person the "mirror." Tell the learners that this game requires "mirrors" to watch the leaders carefully in order to follow all movements exactly. Instruct the leaders to make faces and gestures; challenge those acting as "mirrors" to try to imitate each action as it occurs. After a few moments, direct the partners to switch roles and play the game again.

At the close of "Mirror, Mirror," remind the group that they should model their lives after the example of Saint Margaret of Scotland, a woman who mirrored the love of Jesus to everyone she met.

Offer a snack of shortbread cookies and marmalade. Help the learners understand the symbolism of the treat. Explain that shortbread is a traditional Scottish delicacy. As a way to mirror Jesus' and Margaret's example of serving others, invite each learner to spread marmalade on a piece of shortbread and offer it to another person. Provide water to drink.

Offer a prayer such as "Come, Lord Jesus, be our guest, and let this food to us be blest" before eating the snack.

Intrapersonal Intelligence

Learn

By designing a book cover for a personal bible, participants will understand the reverence Saint Margaret had for Scripture and develop their own appreciation for God's Word.

Locate

Bibles; Glue; Iron; Iron-on interfacing (Optional); Pencils or tailor's chalk; Rulers; Scissors; Scrap paper; Sturdy fabric such as denim, canvas, corduroy, velveteen or drapery material; Trims, such as faux jewels, large sequins, gold cord and braid; Tweezers.

Advance Preparation

Set up an area for ironing.

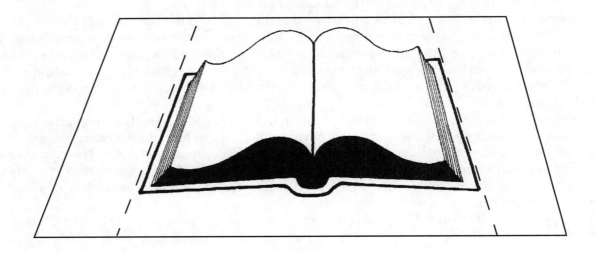

Lead

Margaret shared her love of learning and her knowledge of Christianity with the people of Scotland. She and her husband, King Malcolm, invited Benedictine monks from England and the European continent to settle in Scotland. The monasteries became centers of education for the nearby residents.

Margaret, known as a patroness of learning, loved books and taught others to read. The bible and other books she used were all hand-lettered. Early bookbinders protected books with coverings of leather or precious metals adorned with gemstones.

Explain that each person will make a decorative book cover to protect and beautify a bible. Demonstrate the process for the project.

Choose appropriate fabric; then place an opened bible on top of the cloth. In order to measure the correct size, add about two inches for a hem allowance along the top and bottom edges. Extend the cloth about four inches beyond the right and left sides of the bible to form end flaps.

Set aside the bible until later. Fold over a hem allowance approximately 1-1/2" along the top and bottom edges of the fabric. Make certain that the finished height of the cloth is slightly taller than the height of the bible. Iron the hem with firm pressure and warm enough temperature to give sharp creases to the top and bottom edges of the fabric. If the cloth does not hold a crease, use iron-on interfacing or fabric glue inside the hem. Use care not to shut the four-inch flap opening on each end of the book cover.

Place the spine of the open bible in the center of the creased cloth. Slide the left cover of the bible into the "pocket" formed by the folded hems; then lift the center of the book enough to slide the book's right side into the "pocket" on the opposite end. After adjustments to the fit are made, remove the cover from the bible to add decorative materials. It will be easier to continue if the cover is lying flat on the work surface.

Pre-plan a book cover design on scrap paper or use chalk lines to indicate where decorations will go. Glue trims near the edges of the book cover and embellish the front of it with "jewels" you have collected. Allow the glue to dry before covering the bible.

Provide the supplies and guide the group as they create their book covers. Allow time for the students to display the finished products before they take them home.

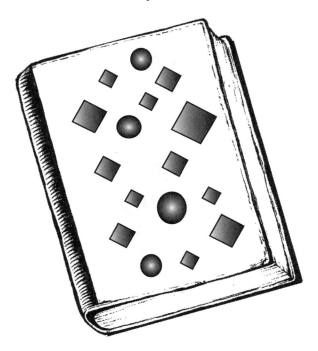

Logical/Mathematical Intelligence

Learn

By following directions to select and organize materials for constructing crowns, participants will demonstrate their understanding of Saint Margaret's story.

Locate

Resource information about Saint Margaret; Construction paper; Glue; Markers; Pencils; Poster board, 2" x 22" per crown; Rulers; Scissors; Stickers, various geometric shapes.

Advance Preparation

Cut poster board into 2" x 22" strips.

Lead

Margaret became the Queen of Scotland when she married King Malcolm. Queen Margaret was a ruler who followed Jesus' example and lived a life of service to her subjects. Saint Margaret's life is a pattern for us to follow as we serve others in Jesus' name.

To help remember the story of this remarkable woman, make poster board crowns with loops containing information about the life of Saint Margaret of Scotland.

Choose a piece of heavy paper to use as the base of the crown. Make sure the strip is long enough to go around the head, with a little extra for overlapping and pasting. Print the words "Saint Margaret of Scotland" on the outside of the paper. Glue the ends of the strip together to form a headband.

Cut several strips of construction paper—the same or different colors—making each one about one inch wide and ten inches long. Write information about Margaret on each piece. Ideas to include might be:

Follower of Jesus
Founded monasteries and churches
Friend of the poor
Lived c. 1045-1093
Loved justice and showed mercy
Mother of 8 children
Queen of Scotland
Spent time in prayer and worship
Treasured books
Wife of King Malcolm

Loop the strips in half without making creases and staple the two ends together inside the headband. Staple one strip right next to the other, until the headband is filled with loops. To make the crown look full, alternate blank strips with strips containing words, if necessary.

Decorate the headband with trims. Apply various shaped stickers or construction paper illustrations, or use markers to draw designs on the crown.

Musical/Rhythmic Intelligence

Learn

By singing the words "My Jesus Gives Life Everlasting" to a familiar tune, participants will discover the message of faith that guided the life of Saint Margaret of Scotland.

Locate

Music for "My Bonnie Lies Over The Ocean" (if not familiar with the classic tune); Words for "My Jesus Gives Life Everlasting."

Lead

Ask how many participants know the song, "My Bonnie Lies Over the Ocean." Sing a few verses to review the tune. Explain that "bonnie" is a Scottish word for "beautiful," and note that this is a familiar Scottish tune. Tie this new knowledge to the life of Saint Margaret of Scotland. Remind the learners that for Saint Margaret, life's greatest beauty would be found in serving others in the name of Christ. Teach the new words by repetition or by displaying them on a chalkboard or an overhead projector. Invite everyone to sing the Scottish tune, "My Bonnie Lies Over The Ocean," with its new words, "My Jesus Gives Life Everlasting," to honor the message of Saint Margaret.

My Jesus Gives Life Everlasting
(Tune: "My Bonnie Lies Over The Ocean")

My Jesus gives life everlasting;
He shows us God's love and God's care.
When you need to know you're forgiven,
Just look in your heart, he'll be there.

Seek him, Seek him
Seek Christ and you'll find him today, today.
Seek him, Seek him,
Seek Christ and you'll find him today.

God asks us to live as examples
Of light in a world that's grown dim.
What we do for each other in service
Jesus says we have done unto him.

Serve him, Serve him.
Serve Christ in your neighbor today, today.
Serve him, serve him.
Serve Christ in your neighbor today.

Naturalist Intelligence

Learn

By playing a game of hopscotch, participants will learn about the geography and the environment of Queen Margaret's Scotland.

Locate

Chalk or masking tape; Duplicating equipment; Examples or pictures of bagpipes, kilts and tartans; Hopscotch Game Answers; Hopscotch Game Questions; Map of Scotland; Paper; Picture of Dunfermline Castle; Stones.

Advance Preparation

Duplicate Hopscotch Game Questions (page 186). Prepare a hopscotch game by drawing the design with chalk or by marking an outline with masking tape.

Lead

Hopscotch sounds like a game that might have originated in Scotland, but that is not so. "To scotch" is an English word that means to score or mark, which is what the players did to create the hopscotch diagram on the ground—they scotched the pattern in the earth with a stone. Originally, the game was associated with life's pilgrimage: The starting point was earth, and the goal was to arrive in heaven by hopping one's way there following the model inscribed for the game.

In the game for this activity, participants will use the hopscotch format as a way to learn about the environment and the geography of Queen Margaret's Scotland. The challenge will be to answer nine questions that correspond to the nine numbers in the hopscotch game. (If possible, display pictures of Dunfermline Castle, a map of Scotland, and examples of the Scottish customs described—bagpipes, kilts and tartans—while the game is being played.)

In preparation for playing the game, share the background information needed to answer the Hopscotch questions, using a script like the following:

Script

Dunfermline, Scotland is the site of the castle where Queen Margaret once lived with her beloved husband, King Malcolm. Dunfermline is located on the bay, which is called a "firth" in the country of Scotland. Scotland is really the northern part of an island. Its southern neighbors are the English. England together with Scotland, Wales, and Ireland make up the British Isles. During Queen Margaret's time, the Scots were a little different than their English neighbors. For one thing, they lived in clans or tribes, and each clan had its own special plaid cloth called a "tartan." Men and boys wore a form of dress called a "kilt." And, they played a very different sounding musical instrument called a "bagpipe."

After the introduction, begin the game by giving a small stone called a "potsie" to the first player. This participant rolls or tosses the stone into the hopscotch design. The player then hops to that square. The leader asks the player the question with the corresponding number on the square. The participant answers, if possible, and then hops back to the starting point. If the player answers the question correctly, the next player must roll the potsie until it lands on a number with an unanswered question. If the first player answered the question incorrectly, then other players may still hop to that location and try again. Continue play until all questions have been answered at least once. As an option, the game may be played cooperatively, with all participants assisting in answering the questions if the one hopping does not know the answer.

Hopscotch Game Questions

1. Margaret was queen of what country?
2. What country is Scotland's neighbor to the south?
3. What is the name of the city where Malcolm and Margaret lived?
4. What do we call the four countries of which Scotland is one part?
5. What is the name of the special clothing that the men of Scotland wear?
6. Each clan in Scotland has a special plaid cloth called what?
7. Name one of the other four countries in the British Isles.
8. What musical instrument are Scottish known to play?
9. What is a bay called in Scotland?

Hopscotch Game Answers

1. Scotland
2. England
3. Dunfermline
4. British Isles
5. Kilts
6. Tartan
7. England, Ireland, or Wales
8. Bagpipes
9. Firth

Verbal/Linguistic Intelligence

Learn

By experiencing a first-person narrative, participants will comprehend biographical information regarding Saint Margaret of Scotland and connect the events of her life to a related Bible story, John 13:4-17, and to the importance of serving others in Jesus' name.

Locate

Bible; Coins or stickers; Costume for "Peasant" Storyteller; Story Script.

Lead

Share the story of Saint Margaret and tell the related Bible story as a first-person narrative. To enhance learning and to make the story memorable, a costumed "peasant" should relate memories about her favorite saint, Margaret of Scotland.

"Peasant" Story Script
(adapted from John 13:4-17)

Greetings! My name is Glenna, which is our Gaelic word for glen or valley. It is a very appropriate name for me, because there have been so many low points in my life. I want to tell you about one time, though, that was a high point for me.

You see, I am just a poor peasant woman who has had to work very hard all of my life. I didn't mind that so much, but one time my health was very poor, and I was unable to grow the food to feed my family. I decided then to go to Dunfermline to the castle because I heard that Queen Margaret would give help to those who really needed it. Have you heard of dear Queen Margaret?

What do you think a queen would be like? Very beautiful and dressed in fancy clothes? Well, Queen Margaret dressed simply. Every day she went out in the streets to wash the feet of the poor and give them money.

When I came to her for help, I couldn't believe it when she knelt before me, unwrapped the filthy rags from my feet, and washed off the caked dirt with her own hands. I felt humbled that so great a lady would do such a thing for the likes of me. The coin she pressed into my hand enabled me to feed my family for a whole year. After that time, I was well again and was able to care for my farm.

Once I heard our pastor tell a story about Jesus. He said that the night before Jesus was to be crucified, he tied a towel around his waist, knelt before each of his disciples, and washed and dried their feet. At first Peter objected to Jesus doing such a thing for him. I can understand how Peter felt. But Jesus explained that those who truly were his disciples must see themselves as the servants of others. When I heard that story, I understood that Queen Margaret was showing us what it means to be a follower of Jesus. Whether we are rich or poor, God cares for us, and God calls us to care for each other.

Ever since my experience with Queen Margaret, I have begun to understand what it truly means to love—it means to share your life with others. Because, you see, it is only what you give away that you really keep. I pray that you will remember this story about our dear Saint Margaret—and Jesus who calls us to be servants of one another.

Have the "peasant" storyteller give each child a coin or a coin sticker to keep.

Visual/Spatial Intelligence

Learn

By designing an original banner, participants will create a visual representation of Margaret's message of service in Jesus' name.

Locate

Acrylic paints for crafts or fabrics; Brushes; Canvas or other firmly woven fabric; Cord; Disposable trays; Dowel rod; Fine point permanent markers; Gesso; Pencils; Picture or pattern of pitcher-basin-towel symbol; Scissors; Sponges; Yardstick.

Advance Preparation

Cut canvas to the desired size. Sew a casing for the dowel rod at the top of the cloth. Prepare the fabric for painting by brushing on a coat of Gesso. Trace or draw the symbol onto the prepared canvas. Fit flat sponges in disposable trays to use as large stamp pads.

Lead

Margaret devoted her life to following Jesus' example of serving others. Work cooperatively to paint a banner depicting a traditional symbol for servanthood: a pitcher, basin and towel based on Jesus' washing of his disciple's feet (John 13:4-17). The design may be painted ahead of the session, or a few artists may be chosen to paint the pre-drawn shapes.

Have each participant add a handprint to the area surrounding the painted symbol. Spread different colors of paint across separate sponges that are arranged in small trays. Invite the learners to press a hand into one of the painted sponges and then onto the canvas. Encourage the painters to place the handprint in an uncrowded area around the symbol. Wash and dry hands. Neatly letter names across each print in order to identify "God's servants."

Allow the paint to dry, slide the rod inside the casing, then add cord to hang the painted banner for all to enjoy.

DECEMBER
SAINT THOMAS BECKET

Biography

Little is known of the early life of Thomas Becket. He is thought to have been born on the feast day of Saint Thomas the Apostle, December 21, 1118, in London. Stories told indicate that he grew to be a tall, handsome, and intelligent man who made friends easily. He was ordained a priest and won the trust of the archbishop of Canterbury with his ability to solve problems and conduct the business of diplomacy well. The archbishop recommended him to King Henry II as an excellent candidate for chancellor of England. The king took an immediate liking to Thomas and the two became fast friends. As chancellor of England, Thomas rose in power and developed a lifestyle that rivaled the king's.

When the archbishop of Canterbury died, King Henry thought of a brilliant idea. He would make his good friend Thomas Becket both chancellor of England and archbishop of Canterbury. That way, the king reasoned, he could hold full power over the church as well as over the state. Thomas begged him not to do this, but the king insisted. Unwillingly, Thomas became archbishop. Henry had no idea that Thomas would take his vows so seriously; he thought their friendship would continue unchanged.

However, Thomas drastically modified his manner of living. He sold his mansion, fine clothes, and rich furnishings and gave the money to the poor. He began to live simply and focus on his commitment to God and to the church. When conflict between earthly and heavenly allegiance arose, Thomas even resigned as Chancellor. As archbishop of Canterbury, Thomas had found a calling even higher than service to the king of England.

The result of Thomas' transformation led him into direct conflict with Henry, who wanted complete control of everything in his kingdom, including the church. When they could not agree over legal matters such as taxation of the church and the rights of the clergy, Henry trumped up charges of embezzlement against Becket. Thomas appealed to the pope and fled England for France to escape the threats on his life. He took refuge in a monastery and stayed there for six years, working behind the scenes to win support for his position and to make peace with Henry.

Finally, he decided to go back to Canterbury, and with the help of the king of France, negotiated with Henry to return. But their conflict continued. When in a rage, Henry hinted to his knights that someone should "rid me of this troublesome priest." On December 29, 1170, four knights rode to Canterbury Cathedral and murdered Thomas at the altar of the church.

The English people and the rest of the world were outraged. Henry II was forced to do public penance. He arranged to have the pope declare Thomas Becket a saint without the usual lengthy process, and he built a shrine to Thomas' memory. Almost immediately people began to flock to Canterbury to the gravesite of the people's priest, Saint Thomas Becket.

Mission

At first, Thomas Becket's mission in life was personal pleasure. He amassed a fortune and was rich in material things. He enjoyed power and used his personal skills to accomplish the king's bidding, thereby winning himself even more wealth and status. When events brought him to the priesthood and made him archbishop of Canterbury, Thomas experienced a transformation. His new mission was to serve God's church and God's people. He discovered the satisfaction of living a simple and holy lifestyle. His energy and personal charm were now directed toward shepherding his flock and protecting the honor of God. Ultimately, he gave his life for his belief that the church should owe its allegiance only to God and not to any earthly king.

Legacy

The life of Thomas Becket illustrates the truth that a deep religious experience can change minds and hearts. Those who find their joy in serving God can turn from one way of life to embrace a new and better way. When we begin to live the faith we profess, others take notice. People responded to Saint

Thomas Becket because they saw him change and benefited from his new generosity of spirit. The legacy of Saint Thomas, then, testifies to the fact that God can change anyone, that God can use human weaknesses to demonstrate Divine Power, and that God offers a life of faith that transcends the importance of anything on earth.

Bodily/Kinesthetic Intelligence

Learn

By playing a game of "Pass It," participants will consider the significance of Thomas Becket's example of a simple life lived for God.

Locate

Objects for the game such as a book, a crown, and a ring; Whistle; Blindfold.

Lead

Thomas Becket spent his life trying to acquire "things," but once he found God, he discovered that true joy only came from what he passed on to others. To illustrate this point, play a game of "Pass It." Instruct the group to form a circle. Display objects such as a book, a crown, or a ring. Connect the objects with the life of Saint Thomas Becket: the book symbolizes that he was a learned man; the crown that he served an earthly king; and the ring, that he was keeper of the Great Seal of England. But none of these achievements were as important to him as serving God and the church.

Explain that at a signal such as a whistle, the group will begin passing one of the symbolic objects. The whistle blower should be blindfolded. Participants should pass the item quickly to the person on their left. The one holding the object when the whistle is blown is "out" and must move to the inside of the circle. Play continues until the last of two players ends up holding the item and is "out." The one remaining with empty hands is deemed the "winner."

Interpersonal Intelligence

Learn

By cooperating to design and display symbols on pennants, participants will recreate medieval pageantry and remember the priority Saint Thomas Becket placed on serving God.

Locate

Carbon paper; Chalk; Examples of coats of arms and monograms; Fabric paints; Felt squares; Glue; Masking tape; Paper towels; Pencils; Plastic lids; Rulers; Scissors; Scrap paper; Small dowel rods or string; Stencil brushes; Stencil paper or card stock.

Lead

As archbishop of Canterbury in medieval England, Thomas Becket was part of many ceremonies and pageants. The church used symbolic letters and pictures to communicate ideas of faith. Banners and tapestries were displayed on festival occasions. Invite participants to work in groups to design their own pennants with pictures or symbols that convey the importance of putting God first in life. Some symbols might include a cross, a crown, a hand pointing heavenward, a number one, or any acceptable representation that the partners can brainstorm together.

Demonstrate the process for making a pennant banner. Try different arrangements on scrap paper; then use carbon paper to transfer the drawing to card stock. Cut out the design to form the stencil.

Choose a felt triangle to make a banner. Use small pieces of tape to secure the stencil to the felt. Dip the brush into the paint, tap excess paint onto a paper towel, then apply the paint through the stencil opening onto the fabric. If more than one color of paint is used, cut a different stencil for each part of the design. Allow the paint to dry.

Glue a dowel directly to the felt along the short end of the triangle or fold and glue the edge to form a casing. Slide the dowel through the casing.

Provide the supplies and guide the process of creating the pennants. Once the groups have completed their pennants, celebrate by orchestrating a procession carrying their designs through hallways or outdoor areas. Play music and sing, cheer, or chant as the group marches through the church or school.

Intrapersonal Intelligence

Learn

By making their own personal seals, participants will relate to experiences from Saint Thomas Becket's life, and like him, choose to seal God's Word in their own hearts.

Locate

Baking tray(s); Bibles; Candles, round stickers, or sealing wax; Examples of seals and signet rings; Glue; Knives; Matches; Modeling compound (Fimo or Sculpy); Nails for incising; Paper, parchment-type and scrap; Pencils or pens; Sandpaper (fine); Stamp pads; Toaster oven or stove with oven; Wooden bases for seals (clothespins, blocks, or spools).

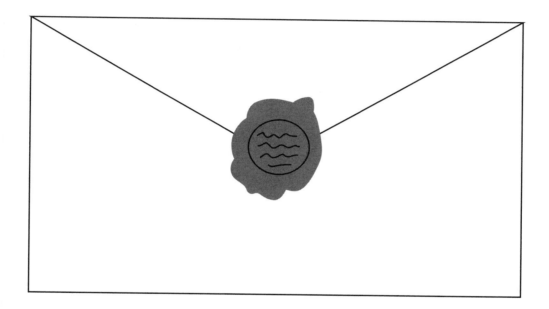

Lead

Long ago, important documents and personal letters were sealed with special signature stamps. The emblem on the seal was a monogram or some other design used to show ownership or authority. A closure, or seal, is formed when a drop of heated wax is used to secure an envelope, parcel or scroll. The seal, or signet, is impressed into the soft wax which then becomes solid as it cools. In early times, signet rings were worn by kings and dignitaries, who used their personal insignias to "seal" important documents.

Both of the high offices held by Saint Thomas Becket—archbishop of Canterbury and lord chancellor of England—required the use of official seals. Thomas wore two rings, one representing his fidelity to an earthly king, Henry II, and the other his loyalty to his heavenly King, God the Father. When he had to choose between his allegiances, Thomas knew where to place his priority—on God and the Church.

Create sealed messages to share an important message that Thomas Becket learned from God's Word. Begin the project by making seals or signets with simple symbols or initials. Distribute modeling clay and direct the group to roll it into a one inch thick "snake." With careful supervision, use a sharp knife to cut the clay into several three-quarter inch diameter circles, then place them on a baking pan. Follow product directions for baking the pieces.

Once the circles are cool, have the students sand any rough or uneven edges. Use sharp nails to incise a symbol or initial into the flat surface of the circles. For easier handling, glue the circles to wooden spools, clothespin heads, or blocks. Remind the group that letters need to be reversed on the signet to print in the proper direction. Test the seals by printing the designs a few times using a stamp pad and scrap paper. If the imprint is not well-defined, widen the incised lines.

Provide Bibles to share and offer each person a piece of parchment-like stationery. Direct the group to locate and copy a verse such as Matthew 22:37 or Mark 9:35b. Encourage each person to learn the verse—to "seal it in his or her heart"—before sealing the paper. Then tell each person to fold his or her paper into thirds. Use candle or sealing wax to make an official emblem. Use extreme caution with this step. Plan to have adults manage dripping wax and matches. With a match, light the end of the candle or wax and place it over the area to be sealed. Melt or drip enough wax to form a small mound across the overlapped edge. Allow the area to cool a little; then press the seal into the center of the soft wax.

For very young children, the "seal" may be a sticker with a stamped emblem in place of the melted wax imprint.

Encourage the participants to share their sealed messages and the story of Saint Thomas Becket with family or friends.

Logical/Mathematical Intelligence

Learn

By following directions to create a rod puppet, participants will review the story of Thomas Becket as they share their information with others.

Locate

Card stock or poster board; Construction paper; Crayons; Glue; Index cards; Markers; Patterns for mitre and vestments; Pencils; Reference books with pictures of vestments; Ribbon; Scissors; Tape; Tongue depressors; Wrapping paper with small pattern.

Lead

Thomas Becket was the son of a well-to-do Norman merchant. He studied liberal arts and law in England and on the Continent. Becket held several church offices when in the service of Theobald, archbishop of Canterbury. King Henry II selected Becket for the powerful position of chancellor of England. Becket then lived in luxury as a member of the court and as a close companion to Henry.

After Theobald died, Henry appointed Becket to become the archbishop of Canterbury. The king planned to use his friend to check the authority of the church. Instead, Becket placed more importance on his responsibility to God and the church than on his loyalty to the king. He resigned the chancellorship and relinquished his wealth to live a simple and more devout life.

Becket's defiance and the king's attempts to control the church resulted in numerous conflicts between the two men. Henry made his displeasure known and as a result, four knights murdered Archbishop Thomas Becket in Canterbury Cathedral. Thomas Becket quickly became known as a martyr of the church and was declared a saint in 1173. His tomb in Canterbury Cathedral was a popular site for pilgrimages.

Make a simple rod puppet to illustrate the story of Thomas Becket as archbishop of Canterbury. Demonstrate the process for making the puppet. Using card stock, copy the basic garment pattern including a head and neck, then cut out the shape. Trace and cut white paper for the archbishop's alb—a basic ankle-length garment of white linen; glue the alb over the card stock form. Trace and cut out the chasuble—a sleeveless, decorative outer vestment worn over the alb. Use patterned gift wrap or draw designs on plain paper to represent needlework; glue over the main garment. Add strips of ribbon or paper to represent the pallium—the symbol of high position in the church. The pallium is in the form of a narrow circle of cloth that goes across the shoulders with a band extending down the front and the back. Glue the pallium to the chasuble.

Cut pieces from skin-colored paper for head and hands. Use markers or crayons to draw the Archbishop's face. Attach the face to the card stock base and glue the hands to the ends of the arms. Trace and cut out the mitre—the tall, ornamental headgear which rise to points in the front and back and is worn by popes and bishops. For a decorative touch, add ribbon trim.

Finish the puppet by fastening it to a stick or strip of sturdy cardboard. On a small card, write out all of the new clothing vocabulary words and glue them to the reverse side of the puppet.

Distribute supplies and direct the process for making the puppets. When they are completed, have the participants use the rod puppets to retell the story of Thomas Becket's life.

Musical/Rhythmic Intelligence

Learn

By sharing a "Syllable Story" based on Mark 9:33-35, participants will associate Jesus' message that "the last shall be first" with the life of Saint Thomas Becket.

Locate

"Last First" Syllable Story Script.

Lead

Thomas Becket came to understand that all of his wealth and power meant nothing in comparison to the satisfaction he found in serving God. He gave away his possessions and wealth to those in need and found—as Jesus taught—that putting himself "last" brought more joy than seeking to be the "first" or the greatest.

Invite everyone to share in retelling the Bible story, Mark 9:33-35, using the "Last First" script and by repeating a two-syllable rhythm. Establish the rhythm by slapping thighs once, clapping hands once, and then snapping fingers of first one hand and then the other. Maintain this rhythmic pattern throughout the entire story. Say one syllable of the first line as thighs are slapped and the second syllable as hands are clapped. The group then repeats the two syllables, one on each snap. Tell the entire narrative in this quick, catchy manner.

"Last First" Syllable Story Script
(adapted from Mark 9:33-35)

Jesus
once heard
his friends
claim that
each would
be first
in Christ's
Kingdom
Someday.

Our Lord
explained
to be
great meant
they must
first choose
last place.

Like them
We must
Care for

Those who
Need us
To show
God's love
On earth.

Naturalist Intelligence

Learn

By exploring the church grounds or a local or parish cemetery and making rubbings of religious symbols, participants will remember the sacrifice of Thomas Becket and understand the meaning of the word "martyr."

Locate

Aluminum foil; Chalk, charcoal, or crayons; Masking tape; Paper (onionskin, parchment, rice paper or shelf paper); Soft, clean cloths.

Lead

Canterbury Cathedral in Canterbury, England has attracted pilgrims since the martyrdom of Thomas Becket. The faithful come to view the burial site of this popular saint to honor and remember him.

Discuss the meaning of the word "martyr": A martyr is a person who sacrifices his or her life for the sake of God's church and for the Christian faith. Saints are remembered on the dates of their death, marking their entrance into eternal life with God. December 29 is Thomas Becket's feast day as that was the date he was murdered at Canterbury Cathedral before the high altar.

During the Middle Ages, one popular activity was making rubbings of a gravestone or a metal alloy tablet known as a "brass." Paper was laid over the surface and rubbed with charcoal or a form of wax called a cobbler's heel ball. A rubbing is similar to a traced image, however, the finished design has a three-dimensional look because of the shading that occurs.

Tell the participants that they are going to make rubbings of crosses or symbols that remind them of the importance of living our lives for God. Encourage them to experience the assurance that, while physical life must come to an end, our belief is in a Creator God who promises us eternal life. Take participants to a local or parish cemetery or the church grounds—and tell them to find markers and symbols that they would like to use for their rubbings. Set the boundaries for the activity, giving directions about reverence for the site and its significance.

Demonstrate the process for the project. Before making a rubbing of any surface, polish it with a clean cloth to eliminate dust or grit. Place a sheet of thin paper over the selected object. Be sure the paper extends beyond the design to protect the area from marks. Tape the edges down to keep the paper from slipping. Rub with the flat side of the charcoal or another material. Move the charcoal across the textured area with firm pressure and enough strokes to reveal the entire design.

Experiment with different papers and rubbing materials. For an interesting variation, press aluminum foil over the designs. Gently rub fingers over and around the raised or engraved areas.

Distribute materials and allow time for each person to make a rubbing. Once the projects are completed, display the rubbings just as they are or cut out and arrange the most interesting textures into a cross-shaped collage.

Verbal/Linguistic Intelligence

Learn

By experiencing a first-person narrative, participants will comprehend biographical information regarding Saint Thomas Becket and connect the events of his life to a related Bible story, Mark 9:33-35, and to the importance of placing God first in life.

Locate

Bible; Costume for "Knight" Storyteller; Heart stickers or symbols; Story script.

Lead

Share the story of Thomas Becket and tell the related Bible story, Mark 9:33-35, as a first-person narrative. To enhance learning and to make the story memorable, a costumed "Knight" should enter the gathering and relate memories about his favorite Saint, Thomas Becket.

"Knight's" Story Script
(adapted from Mark 9:33-35)

Greetings! My name is Edwin, well actually, Sir Edwin since I was knighted by his Majesty, King Henry III. "Edwin" means "valuable friend" which is what a knight is meant to be. Knights must take the oath of chivalry, a time when we pledge to uphold honor, to protect those weaker than ourselves, and to swear our loyalty to God, the church, and the King of our land. I spent many years training to become a knight, and it is my good pleasure to be here today to tell you about someone who discovered what it means to be a valuable friend, my own patron saint, Thomas Becket.

Becket was a friend and chancellor to King Henry II, but that was before Becket discovered something more important in life than serving an earthly power. As the king's chancellor, he had wealth and a commanding position in one of the most powerful countries on earth, England. Becket was a loyal friend to King Henry. But then Henry made Becket the archbishop of Canterbury, so he was also the most powerful leader of the Church in England. And guess what friend Becket discovered when he became archbishop—Becket discovered God! I would say that's a valuable friend!

For the first time in his life, Thomas Becket found satisfaction in living—not by being powerful and rich in monetary wealth, but by sharing what he had with others. One of his first official acts after he was appointed as archbishop was to give away his gold, his fancy clothes, in fact everything he had spent a lifetime collecting. He discovered that in giving to others, he had found a greater reward and blessing than he had ever before experienced.

You see, Thomas Becket learned what Jesus taught when he was on earth with his disciples: to be great means to be a servant. Even the disciples misunderstood at first what Jesus represented. One day they were arguing about who was going to be the greatest in Christ's kingdom. They wanted the position that Becket enjoyed—to be the Lord's most important friend. Jesus set them straight. To be important in the kingdom of God is to be a servant of others, or as Jesus said, "If any one would be first, he must be last of all and servant of all."

I am sad to say that it was a group of King Henry II's knights who killed Thomas Becket as he knelt before God's altar in the Canterbury Cathedral. Those knights must not have realized that they owed their allegiance to an even higher king than King Henry. Their hearts were not open to God and to serving others like Saint Thomas Becket was.

As a knight myself, I want to be loyal to my king. But I also want to remember that my heart's true allegiance must first be to God. (Display heart symbol.) And if I am to be great in God's kingdom, I must serve those around me. Remember to keep your hearts turned toward God and toward each other. Then you will be on your way toward living like a true knight—a valuable friend of God's.

At the conclusion, have the knight give each child a heart sticker or a heart symbol to keep.

Visual/Spatial Intelligence

Learn

By creating their own stained glass designs, participants will review the architectural features of Canterbury Cathedral and its role in the life of Saint Thomas Becket.

Locate

Construction paper, black; Glue sticks; Markers, black; Paper, thin white such as onionskin or tracing paper; Pattern for Gothic arch; Pencils; Puff paint or other craft paint in tubes with fine nozzles; Reference materials on Canterbury Cathedral and its stained glass windows; Rulers; Scissors; Tissue paper, various colors.

Lead

On December 29, 1170, Thomas Becket was murdered in Canterbury Cathedral. After Pope Alexander canonized the martyred archbishop in 1173, it became a popular site for religious pilgrimages.

The architectural style of the cathedral in Canterbury, England is primarily English Gothic, also known as English Perpendicular because of the emphasis on vertical lines. The church's interior has a vaulted ceiling and an elaborate arrangement of columns and arches. Canterbury Cathedral has a tall tower with spires, called a rood tower, rising from the front part of the nave at the altar-point.

Stained glass windows are one of the outstanding features of Canterbury Cathedral. Many of the windows tell stories of the life and the miracles of Saint Thomas: for example, miracles associated with a man who was cured of a toothache; a man who gave thanks after being cured of leprosy; and a priest who was cured of paralysis. In addition to information about Saint Thomas, there are accounts of everyday life: young boys throwing stones at large, green frogs; a boy who has fallen into the water; and village scenes.

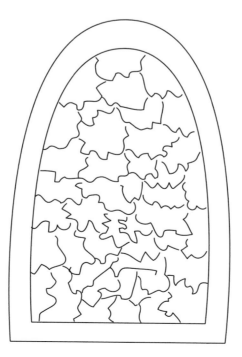

Try the art of "stained glass making." Demonstrate the process for the students. Select a piece of white paper and use a ruler to draw a two-inch margin around the edge. Think about the subject matter for the design, then sketch it with pencil inside the margin lines. Keep the figures and objects simple, without too many tiny details. Trace and cut colored tissue paper to fit over different shapes on the drawing. When most of the shapes are cut, cover the white background paper with glue from a glue stick. Glue the tissue paper as flat and as smooth as possible. Allow the collage to dry. Outline the pencil lines showing through the tissue colors to indicate leading in stained glass windows. Use black marker or a thin trail of dark craft paint that comes in a tube with a pointed nozzle designed for tracing lines.

While the marker or paint lines are drying, use the pattern of a Gothic arch to cut a simple frame from black construction paper. Glue the frame to the margin around the tissue collage to give the window a finished look.

Provide supplies and guide the process of creating the stained glass windows. When the projects are completed, display the creations where light will show through. Remind the students to think about the beautiful stained glass windows in the English Gothic Cathedral of Canterbury.

ACTIVITY INDEX

Methods

Architecture

- Bridges (Saint Catherine of Siena: Naturalist) 71
- Building Blocks (Saint Francis of Assisi: Logical/Mathematical) 166
- Scavenger Hunt (Saint Peter: Interpersonal) 97
- Stained Glass Window (Saint Thomas Becket: Visual/Spatial) 205

Art

- Bible/Book Cover (Saint Margaret of Scotland: Intrapersonal) 180
- Bible Verse Viewer (James & Jesus) (Saint James the Greater: Logical/Mathematical) 117
- Book/Prayers (Stitched) (Saint Patrick: Intrapersonal) 48
- Candles (Saint Hildegard of Bingen: Intrapersonal) 147
- Clay (Saint Catherine of Siena: Bodily/Kinesthetic) 63
- Collage (Photographs/Psalm 27) (Saint Joan of Arc: Naturalist) 88
- Crayon Resist (Mandala) (Saint Hildegard of Bingen: Visual/Spatial) 155
- Crest (Saint Joan of Arc: Intrapersonal) 83
- Cross/Cube ("When I Survey The Wondrous Cross") (Saint Clare: Musical/Rhythmic) 135
- Crown (Saint Margaret of Scotland: Logical/Mathematical) 182
- Diorama ("All Creatures of Our God and King"/Canticle of the Sun) (Saint Francis of Assisi: Musical/Rhythmic) 168
- Dove (Hand Shape) (Saint Scholastica: Naturalist) 38
- Faith Tree (Mentors) (Saint Clare: Interpersonal) 131
- Fingerprint Heart (Saint Agnes: Musical/Rhythmic) 23
- Heart Pocket (Saint Catherine of Siena: Intrapersonal) 66
- Metal Tooled Celtic Cross (Saint Patrick: Visual/Spatial) 58
- Mobile (Crown of Gold/Crown of Thorns) (Saint Catherine of Siena: Visual/Spatial) 75
- Mosaic (Paper/Symbols) (Saint Peter: Visual/Spatial) 108
- Palm Palms (Saint Clare: Naturalist) 137
- Picture Frame (Shells) (Saint James the Greater: Naturalist) 120
- Postcard (Saint Catherine of Siena: Interpersonal) 64
- Prayer Journal (Spontaneous Prayer) (Saint Scholastica: Intrapersonal) 35
- Prayer Prompter (Saint Scholastica: Interpersonal) 33
- Rock Garden (Saint Peter: Naturalist) 105
- Rubbings (Symbols) (Saint Thomas Becket: Naturalist) 201
- Ruler (Saint Scholastica: Logical/Mathematical) 36
- Sealed Message (Bible Verse) (Saint Thomas Becket: Intrapersonal) 195
- Stained Glass Window (Saint Thomas Becket: Visual/Spatial) 205
- Story Board (Saint Scholastica: Visual/Spatial) 40
- Timeline (Saint Joan of Arc: Logical/Mathematical) 84
- Triptych (Saint Patrick: Logical/Mathematical) 51
- Visual Art (Saint Agnes: Visual/Spatial) 27

Banner/Textiles

- Banner (Footprints) (Saint James the Greater: Visual/Spatial) 124
- Banner (Servanthood Theme) (Saint Margaret of Scotland: Visual/Spatial) 188
- Bible/Book Cover (Saint Margaret of Scotland: Intrapersonal) 180

- Rod Puppet (Plastic Tub) (Saint Hildegard of Bingen: Naturalist) 151
- Rod Puppet (Tube) (Saint Clare: Bodily/Kinesthetic) 128

Storytelling

- Action Story: "Ask, Seek, Knock" (Saint Patrick: Bodily/Kinesthetic) 45
- Action Story: "Jesus Serves" (Saint Margaret of Scotland: Bodily/Kinesthetic) 177
- Echo Story: "The Transfiguration" (Saint James the Greater: Bodily Kinesthetic) 113
- First-Person Story—Benedictine Monk (Saint Scholastica: Verbal/Linguistic) 39
- First-Person Story—Biographer (Raymond of Capua) (Saint Catherine of Siena: Verbal/Linguistic) 73
- First-Person Story—Father (Saint Agnes: Verbal/Linguistic) 26
- First-Person Story—Fishmonger's Wife (Saint Peter: Verbal/Linguistic) 107
- First-Person Story—Franciscan Brother (Saint Francis of Assisi: Verbal/Linguistic) 171
- First-Person Story—Innkeeper (Saint James the Greater: Verbal/Linguistic) 122
- First-Person Story—Knight (Saint Thomas Becket: Verbal/Linguistic) 203
- First-Person Story—Minstrel (Saint Patrick: Verbal/Linguistic) 56
- First-Person Story—Mother (Saint Clare: Verbal/Linguistic) 138
- First-Person Story—Peasant (Saint Margaret of Scotland: Verbal/Linguistic) 187
- First-Person Story—Sexton (Saint Joan of Arc: Verbal/Linguistic) 89
- First-Person Story—Sister (Saint Hildegard of Bingen: Verbal/Linguistic) 153
- Guided Meditation (Jesus/Bridge) (Saint Catherine of Siena: Naturalist) 71
- Guided Meditation (Jesus/Peter/Shore) (Saint Peter: Intrapersonal) 99
- *Lectio Divina* (Saint Clare: Intrapersonal Intelligence) 133
- Literary Circles (Books/Movies) (Saint Joan of Arc: Interpersonal) 81
- Rhythm Story: "Peter Walks On Water" (Saint Peter: Bodily/Kinesthetic) 95
- Scripture Script (Christmas Story) (Saint Francis of Assisi: Interpersonal) 161
- Story Board (Saint Scholastica: Visual/Spatial) 40
- Syllable Story: "Last First" (Saint Thomas Becket: Musical/Rhythmic) 199

Multiple Intelligences

Bodily/Kinesthetic

- Action Story—"Ask, Seek, Knock" (Saint Patrick) 45
- Action Story—"Jesus Serves" (Saint Margaret of Scotland) 177
- Body Puppet (Saint Joan of Arc) 79
- Charades (Saint Hildegard of Bingen) 144
- Clay (Saint Catherine of Siena) 63
- Echo Story—"The Transfiguration" (Saint James the Greater) 113
- "Pass It" Game (Saint Thomas Becket) 192
- Relay (Partners) (Saint Scholastica) 31
- Rhythm Story—"Peter Walks On Waters" (Saint Peter) 95
- "Simple Gifts" Dance (Saint Francis of Assisi) 159
- "Truth or Fable" Game (Saint Agnes) 17
- Tube Puppets (Saint Clare of Assisi) 128

Interpersonal

- Architectural Scavenger Hunt (Saint Peter) 97
- Banners and Tapestry (Saint Thomas Becket) 193
- Cinquain Poetry (Saint Hildegard of Bingen) 146
- Drama/Scripture Scripts (Christmas Story) (Saint Francis of Assisi) 161
- Faith Tree (Mentors) (Saint Clare) 131
- "I'm Going To Ireland" Game (Saint Patrick) 47
- "Jeopardy" (Saint Agnes) 18
- Literary Circles (Books/Music) (Saint Joan of Arc) 81
- Mirror, Mirror Game (Saint Margaret of Scotland) 179
- Postcard (Saint Catherine of Siena) 64
- Prayer Prompter (Saint Scholastica) 33
- Snack (Bread, Cheese, Grapes, Olives) (Saint James the Greater) 115
- Snack (Gummi Snakes; Shamrock-Shaped Finger Gelatin) (Saint Patrick) 47
- Snack (Marmalade, Shortbread) (Saint Margaret of Scotland) 179
- Telephone Game (Saint James the Greater) 115

Intrapersonal

- Bible/Book Cover (Saint Margaret of Scotland) 180
- Book/Prayers (Stitched) (Saint Patrick) 48
- Candles (Saint Hildegard of Bingen) 147
- Crest (Saint Joan of Arc) 83
- Essay (Saint Agnes) 20
- Guided Meditation/Journal (Jesus/Peter/Shore) (Saint Peter) 99
- Heart Pocket (Saint Catherine of Siena) 66
- *Lectio Divina* (Saint Clare of Assisi) 133
- "Lord, Make Me An Instrument Of Your Peace" (Peace Prayer) (Saint Francis of Assisi) 164
- Names (James/Them) (Saint James the Greater) 116
- Prayer Journal (Spontaneous Prayer) (Saint Scholastica) 35
- Sealed Message (Bible Verse) (Saint Thomas Becket) 195

Logical/Mathematical

Musical/Rhythmic

Naturalist

Verbal/Linguistic

Scripture

Old Testament

New Testament

- John 20:1-18—Mary Magdalene
Saint Catherine of Siena   73
Biographer

About the Authors

Phyllis Vos Wezeman

Phyllis Wezeman is president of Active Learning Associates, Inc., and director of Christian Nurture at a downtown parish in South Bend, Indiana. Phyllis has served as adjunct faculty in the Education Department at Indiana University and the Department of Theology at the University of Notre Dame. She has also taught at the Saint Petersburg (Russia) State University of Pedagogical Art and the Shanghai (China) Teacher's University. Phyllis, who holds an M.S. in Education, is a recipient two "Distinguished Alumnus Awards" from Indiana University and the Catholic Library Association's Aggiornamento Award. Author or co-author of numerous books and articles, this is her fourth publication for Ave Maria Press. Phyllis and her husband, Ken, have three children and three grandsons.

Anna L. Liechty

Anna Liechty is a National Board Certified teacher and co-chair of a High School English Department. She has also worked in religious education, teaching all levels, directing Sunday morning and youth programming, consulting with congregations about their educational ministry, and writing a wide variety of religious education materials. She serves as vice president of Active Learning Associates, Inc. Anna lives in Plymouth, Indiana, with her husband Ron, a retired pastor. They have five children and ten grandchildren.